Norfolk Island Parrakeet
(Cyanoramphus   cooki)

NEW ZEALAND PARRAKEETS
(Kakarikis)

NEW ZEALAND
PARRAKEETS
(Kakarikis)

Dr J Batty

NIMROD PRESS LTD
15 The Maltings
Turk Street
Alton, Hants, GU34 1DL

NIMROD PRESS LTD
15 The Maltings
Turk Street
Alton, Hants, GU34 1DL

CONTENTS

ILLUSTRATIONS

PREFACE

Kakarikis are fascinating birds with behaviour which is not typically characteristic of parrakeets. They are curious birds which appear to like human companionship and thrive quite well in an aviary. They are not suitable subjects for a small cage.

They have had a chequered history, being slaughtered by farmers and hunters and then by rats and other predators. In addition, also in their natural habitat, they have had to contend with harsh conditions including cold and very wild weather.

Inevitably this has taken its toll and a point was reached when they appeared doomed and would become, like the dodo, an extinct species. In fact, they seemed destined for a worse fate because they were almost forgotten even by the people of New Zealand.

After a gap of many years enthusiastic breeders such as E. J. Boosey, the Marquess of Tavistock and Sydney Porter tried to stimulate an interest in these birds. Today they exist in quite reasonable numbers and appear to be all set for becoming one of the more popular species of parrakeets.

This book has been produced to stimulate further interest in New Zealand Parrakeets. In writing it I have consulted many books and journals. Comments and experiences of other breeders would be appreciated. The problem with a revival is that there are all too few articles or books on the subject in question. Unlike the keeping of budgerigars, canaries and other popular birds, time has been too short to establish the best practices.

In writing this concise book on the New Zealand Parrakeets I am mindful that difficulties exist on precise colours. Because some of the wild species have virtually disappeared and the domesticated species have been cross-bred for colours there is no knowing what are the exact colours.

One of the anomalies is that yellow-fronted have crimson-red frontal bands, but orange-fronted have an orange frontal area. In fact, in practice it may be reddish orange. All this is fairly academic because only yellow-and red-fronted appear to exist. *

With Kakarikis common sense management appears to be the order of the day. Provide adequate shelter, a balanced diet and interesting surroundings and these birds will thrive and breed. Experiment with fruit, green stuff and basic seed to see what they like.

Some fanciers feed daily, others give sufficient mixed seed for a few days and then supplement with fruit and greens on a regular basis. There is no hard and fast rule; so long as the birds are happy and thriving a flexible approach is acceptable. Overfeeding should also be avoided.

My thanks to Susan Lawson who photographed the birds in colour.

June, 1989   J. Batty

* The terminology of Red–Fronted and Yellow–Fronted is that normally used, but I am inclined to think that Red–Crowned and Yellow–Crowned is more appropriate and would avoid confusion.

Red Fronted Kakariki
Note red spot behind eye (not on yellow-fronted)

Kakariki lacking blue pigment

1

PARROTS
AND
PARROT-LIKE BIRDS

Grey Parrot

Blue-fronted Amazon

Ring -necked Parrakeet

Macaw

Hooded Parrakeet

Rosy faced Love bird

Rose-breasted Cockatoo

Black-headed Caique

Fig.1-1 **Some of the Parrot Family**

CHAPTER 1
PARROTS AND PARROT-LIKE BIRDS

THE FAMILY GROUP

Parrots belong to the order *Psittaciformes* and are grouped into the family known as *Psittacidae*. Within this family there are different groups of species (around 330) which are further broken into around 60 genera.

A further classification is the division into *sub-families* such as:*

1. NESTORINAE — covers the Kaka and Kea parrots from New Zealand.

2. STRIGOPINAE — includes the Owl Parrot or Kakapo.

3. CYCLOPSITTACINAE† – a genus PSITTACULIROST-RIS which contains five species originating from New Guinea, dwarf-like (around 4 to 7 inches, 10 to 18cm) and believed to be related to the Lories.

4. PLATYCERCINAE which covers a wide range of species (29) which include the Rosellas.

5. CACATUINAE — covers the cockatoos of which there are some 16 species. It includes the popular Cockatiels.

6. MICROPSITTINAE which includes six species of pygmy parrots. These diminutive birds (around 4in (10cm)) which use their feathers to support themselves when climbing trees.

7. LORIINAE which includes around 60 species of brush tongued parrots known as Lories and Lorikeets which feed on liquids (nectars) rather than seeds.

8. PSITTACINAE consisting of the bulk of the parrots

*This classification is not standardised so variations will be found.
†May be grouped with sub-family 6.

ranging from quite small birds such as Love Birds to the giants such as Amazon and Macaw Parrots.

The classification of a particular bird may be changed and it would then be included in its new group.

Because of the need to have an international language for describing birds Latin names are used as well as the equivalent in the language of the country in which they are kept. This can lead to rather complicated descriptions being used, but is obviously the only practical way.

PARROT FAMILY UNIQUE

Parrots and parrot-like birds possess features which are unique:

1. Beak which is hinged, the upper mandible being attached to the forehead in a manner which allows great movement and flexibility for cracking seeds and nuts.

2. Lower mandible is light, thin and deep which cuts into the food. It is shorter than the upper, curved mandible.

3. Foot of the parrot is completely zygodactyle (two toes pointing forward and two back) and prehensile (capable of grasping), thus allowing great mobility, being able to climb vertical posts or trees, also using its beak in the process.

4. The fleshy tongue is thick and muscular and allows the bird to taste food and manipulate it within the beak, discarding husks or pods which are not eaten.

Obviously this summary does not cover the multitude of varieties which exist. Special mention must be made of the Lories and Lorikeets which possess a tongue containing a brush of strong hairs used for procuring nectar food from flowers.

2

HISTORY OF
THE
CYANORAMPHUS PARRAKEETS

The Red-fronted New Zealand Parrakeet.

This is another very nice bird, which I am sorry to hear is becoming rather scarce in its own country, and is, consequently, but seldom imported now. Like the rest of the Parrots and Parrakeets that have their home in the "Southern Britain", this species is mainly terrestrial in its habits, hence its tarsi are long and it hops and runs on the ground with much grace and agility, but it is an indifferent percher. It has a curious trick of scratching with its feet on the ground after the manner of the Gallinaceae.

Dr W.T. Greene *Feathered Friends – Old and New*, L. Upcott Gill, London, 1896.

Dr Greene was one of the very early writers on aviculture.

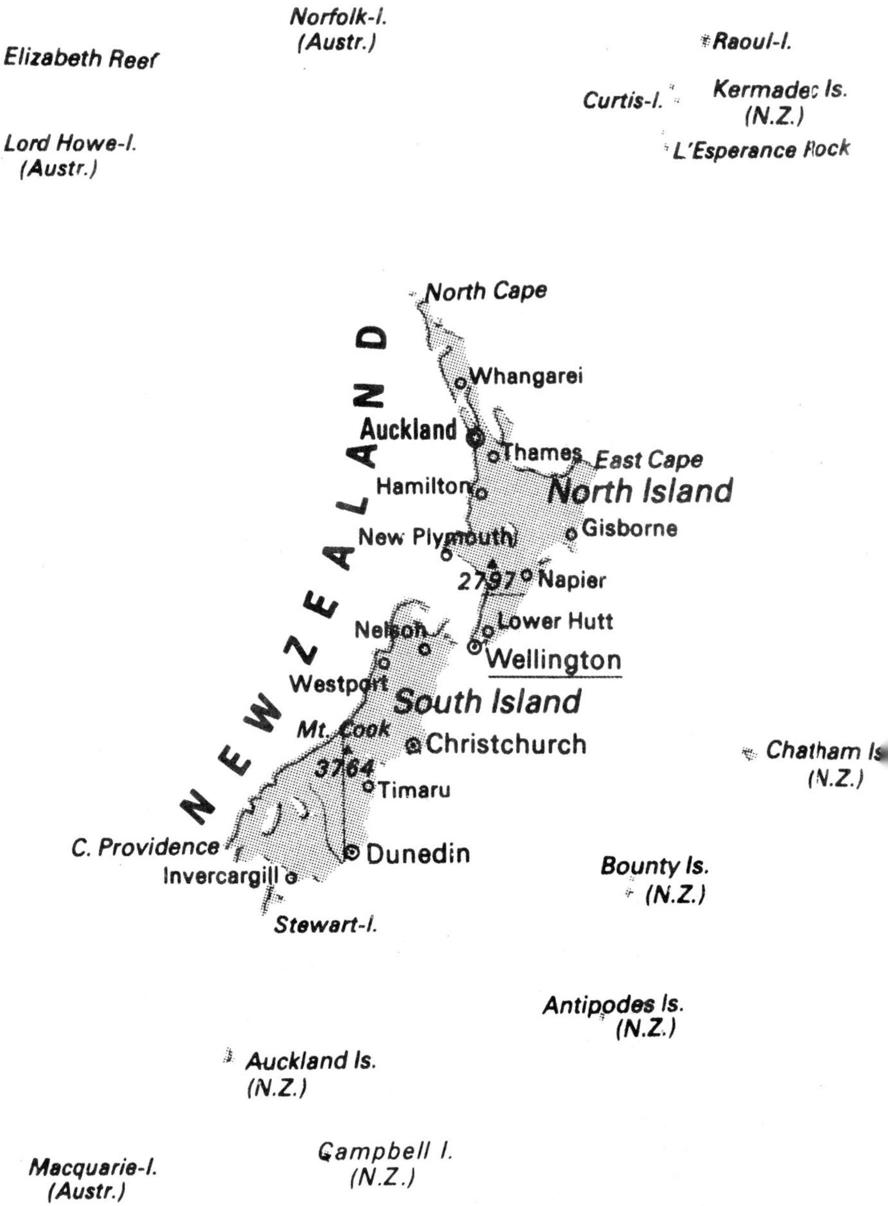

Elizabeth Reef

Norfolk-I.
(Austr.)

*Raoul-I.

Curtis-I.

Kermadec Is.
(N.Z.)

L'Esperance Rock

Lord Howe-I.
(Austr.)

North Cape

NEW ZEALAND

Whangarei

Auckland

Thames East Cape

Hamilton

North Island

New Plymouth

Gisborne

2797 Napier

Nelson

Lower Hutt

Westport

Wellington

South Island

Mt. Cook

Christchurch

Chatham Is.
(N.Z.)

3764

Timaru

C. Providence

Dunedin

Invercargill

Bounty Is.
(N.Z.)

Stewart-I.

Antipodes Is.
(N.Z.)

Auckland Is.
(N.Z.)

Macquarie-I.
(Austr.)

Campbell I.
(N.Z.)

Figure 2-1   Distribution Map of the New Zealand Parrakeets

CHAPTER 2
HISTORY OF THE CYANORAMPHUS PARRAKEETS

EARLY HISTORY

We are not always aware of the work done by aviculturists in preserving the New Zealand Parrakeet from extinction. Yet in these attractive Parrakeets we have a genus which has been brought "back to life" by the perseverance of a few dedicated bird keepers.

SETTING THE SCENE

Writing just over 55 years ago Sydney Porter, a much travelled aviculturist, wrote a series of articles in *The Aviculturist Magazine.* He explained the position with the *Cyanorhamphus* at that stage and parts of his work are now produced:

NOTES ON THE CYANORHAMPHUS *
PARRAKEETS

The Cyanorhamphus Parrakeets form a very distinct genus and are confined to the New Zealand region; though some members are found on far distant islands which are no doubt the last remaining outposts of some vast continent which was submerged beneath the Southern Pacific Ocean many eons ago.

These Parrakeets vary in size from slightly larger than a Budgerigar, in the case of the New Zealand Alpine Parrakeet (*Cyanorhamphus malherbie*), to as large as a Pennant in *Cyanorhamphus cooki* from Norfolk Island, which is the largest of the genus.

In colour they are not particularly striking, being more or less of a uniform grass green marked with either red or yellow, and blue. These Parrakeets are remarkable for the fact that they inhabit regions far from the tropics and several species are confined to desolate, bleak, and often treeless islands, where the species have become, owing to the absence of trees, practically terrestrial.

*Note the slightly different spelling from the modern version Cyanoramphus.

Unfortunately, civilized man has dealt very hardly with these birds and several species are now extinct; others are on the verge of extermination, while none are in a flourishing condition. The two commonest species, which were confined to the mainland and which were found in great abundance before the advent of the white man to the shores of New Zealand, are now greatly reduced in numbers and are found only in the most remote forested districts as well as on several of the islands off the coast.

The two species mentioned, the Red-fronted Parrakeets and the Yellow-fronted Parrakeets, were very well known to British avi-culturists forty* or more years ago, and were bred with comparative ease in the aviaries of several bird-keepers. But it was the same with these as with any other bird which was comparatively easy to obtain, people did not bother to breed them and they just died out. Now these interesting species will never grace our aviaries again.†

THE ANTIPODES ISLAND PARRAKEET (*Cyanorhamphus unicolor*)

This unique Parrakeet is confined to a tiny island far distant from New Zealand, and well on the way to the chill Antarctic Ocean. Very few specimens have been brought away alive. Buller, the great New Zealand naturalist, had several; the Zoological Society had one or two many years ago; in fact, the type was described from a bird in the possession of the Society, the habitat of which was then unknown, and recently the Marquess of Tavistock possessed a single example. This bird, which is doubtless the last which will ever reach these shores, was procured by a sailor from a small ship which stopped at the island. The bird was knocked over with a stick by the man on the shore, which shows how fearless this species is in a wild state.

I had great hopes of visiting the lonely island which forms the home of this strange Parrakeet, for I thought that I might be able to get as a passenger on the small Government steamer which once a year visits the islands in the far south in search of castaways and also to replenish the food store on the islands which is kept in case any unfortunate individuals get shipwrecked there. But alas! I found out from the High Commissioner in London that, owing to means of economy, the steamer no longer visited the islands in the borders of the Antarctic, and the would-be castaways are now left to their fate!

Every inquiry possible was made, and I found that the only means of getting there was to charter a special ship, which would have to be of a large tonnage owing to the tempestuous seas. The price asked was £500, which, needless to say, was quite beyond my means, so I reluctantly had to give up the project.

I very much regret to say that I fear the numbers of this bird have been greatly reduced by the members of a certain American expedition which has been ravaging the islands of the Pacific for several years and almost wiping out whole species of birds. This

*Editorial Note: this would be at the end of the 19th Century.
†Fortunately he was wrong! They are still in existence but only due to the dedication of pioneer breeders.

expedition collected many skins of this species, and from what I heard of the brutal slaughter by the members of the expedition of this isolated type its fate is certainly in the balance.

The death knell of various rare island species is certainly sounded when such expeditions as these pursue their depredations unchecked. Instead of assisting ornithological research they appear to be hampering it, at least for future generations. They have left such a name behind them that they will never be allowed to collect again in many of the British Islands, especially New Zealand.

During my visit to Steward Island and the outlying islands I saw something of the terrible seas of those parts, and it is little wonder that few ships ever call at the bleak islands in the far south. The great marvel is that a Parrot has been able to adapt itself to such severe conditions as prevail on the island on which it is found. As mentioned before, it is very unlikely that the bird will ever be seen alive again by aviculturists in Europe, for which the stopping of the Govenment steamer and the total closing of the seal-killing season there is no reason for any ship to brave the terrible gales which rage in those seas.

The Antipodes Island Parrakeet is completely terrestrial and lives on the ground amongst the tussock grass, feeding upon the seeds of the grass. The very boisterous winds have made flight almost impossible for this bird, and it is very feeble on the wing, though it can run and climb about the rocks with the greatest agility.

W.R.B.Oliver, who has seen the bird in its native haunts, tells us in his book *New Zealand Birds* that this Parrakeet "is a ground bird which walks and climbs but seldom takes wing. It is found among the tussocks and scrub and also on the rocks along the shore including the breeding places of the Penguins. It is quite fearless and makes a low chattering sound as it walks about. It breeds in holes in the chick matted bases of the grass tussocks".

A short description of the home of this unique bird may be of interest, and the following is an extract from a letter from the High Commissioner of New ·Zealand in London: "The Antipodes Islands lie some 490 miles east-south-east from the southernmost point of Stewart Island . . . The largest island is known as Antipodes Island, and measures 4 miles from east to west and 2 miles from north to south. At its highest point it reaches an elevation of 1,300 feet. The coast is rocky and precipitous, with steep slopes covered with tussock rising from the tops of the cliffs to the high land in the centre of the island. . . . The tussock grows from 4 to 6 feet in height in many parts and so close together that it is a matter of difficulty to force one's way through it. There are no trees on the island, but some patches of shrubs, particularly in the shallow gullies, where rank growth of fern are also found. In addition to the various seabirds which nest there, the island is noted for a small Green Parrakeet, which is found fairly plentifully amongst the tussock grass."

The weather on this isolated island is far from ideal, terrible gales and storms sweep over it in the winter time from the Antarctic and make it anything but a desirable place for a Parrakeet to live on. But in spite of this it seems to have been able to fight the elements and hold its own until the coming of the arch enemy of all feather life, Man, who seems to have made short work with this highly specialized and interesting species. The Antipodes Island Parrakeet is about 14 inches in length and of a uniform yellowish grass-green, with the primary coverts and the outer edges of the primaries bright blue. The legs are particularly long and eminently suited for the terrestrial life which the bird leads.

Some of these birds were transferred to Kapiti Island in 1907, but there were none there when I visited it. Highly specialized animals hardly ever thrive when transferred from their own habitat to another. There is certainly no tussock on Kapiti on which the birds could feed.

Buller says: "My captive birds seemed perfectly happy although caged when adult. They partook freely of maize and oats, also of apples, grapes, figs, and, indeed, ripe fruit of any kind. They could bite severely, as I soon learned to my cost . . . Although captured as adult birds they readily take to confinement and do not fret, as most other birds do, at being caged. I have noticed that this species has a habit of resting at night in an upright position, holding on to the wires of its cage by both bill and feet."

THE MACQUARIE ISLAND PARRAKEET (*Cyanorhamphus n. erythrotis*)

Macquarie Island will no doubt be better known to readers as the original "Penguin Island". It is one of those tiny islands which lie far off the coast of New Zealand and well on the way to the Antarctic. It was until recently the scene of the most terrible and disgusting slaughter of the Penguins, when every year tens of thousands of these hapless birds were driven into great vats or digesters to be boiled down alive for the sake of a cheap commercial oil used mainly for the greasing of ropes, as it was a trifle less in cost than mineral oil. On this island lived a small Parrakeet of the *Cyanorhamphus* group, a bird like the Antipodes Island Parrakeet, which was particularly terrestrial in its habits, more from force of circumstances than anything else, as there are no trees on the island, it being too bleak and wind-swept.

This Parrakeet, like the last, derived its sustenance from the seeds of the tussock grass and also nested under the clumps of the same grass. A scientific expedition which called at this island within recent years failed to find the bird, so had reluctantly to come to the conclusion that it was extinct.

Some time afterwards I met one of the professional Penguin killers from Macquarie Island, and he told me that the Parrakeet had disappeared prior to his advent there some years before the War. There is little doubt that this bird was exterminated through the agency of cats, which were brought by the Penguin killers in the very early days and which were left to fend for themselves when the men left in the winter. These animals have greatly increased and still take a great toll of the bird life. The Macquarie Island Parrakeet is similar to the Red-fronted Parrakeet, but is of a more yellowish green, especially on the under parts, and there is very little blue on the wings.

THE RED-FRONTED PARRAKEET (*Cyanorhamphus novaezelandiae*)

There is no doubt that in the course of time both this bird and its ally, the Yellow-fronted Parrakeet, will vanish from the mainland of New Zealand. Fortunately it will not vanish from the face of the earth so long as the New Zealand Government still retain the Little Barrier Island, Kapiti Island, and the islands off Stewart Island as sanctuaries for New Zealand's much persecuted bird life. On these islands the birds are numerous, especially the Red-fronted. The latter birds are also extremely common on some more very small islands, the names of which had perhaps better not be mentioned.

Once exceedingly common, the Red-fronted Parrakeets were to be seen in flocks of thousands; now on the mainland they are restricted to a few very remote localities. On my arrival in New Zealand I spent a considerable time in searching for these birds, and at last tracked down a small colony in the forest reserve of Lake Waikaremoana. In every other locality I was told that the Parrakeets were very plentiful forty years or more ago, but had now quite disappeared and were now never seen.

Like most of New Zealand's birds, it is dependent on the forests for its food, and it is intolerant of any interference on the part of man. For wherever timber-felling operations are started prior to the burning of the forest, the birds quickly disappear. Many years ago Parrot shooting was a favourite "sport" with the colonists, and this no doubt helped to reduce the numerical strength of the birds to a great degree.

This Parrakeet is very rarely kept in captivity in New Zealand now. When I was first in New Zealand I did hear of one, but when I tracked it down it proved to be a White Cockatoo! We shall never see this interesting species in our aviaries again, except perhaps an odd one or two now and again which happens to be smuggled out of the country, for the New Zealand Government would rather see fifty perish in a forest fire than a single pair leave the country for breeding purposes.

To show the great rarity of this bird on the mainland, many people who were interested in birds had never seen it and most ordinary people had never even heard of it. The birds which I did manage to see on the mainland were exceedingly timid and it was impossible to get within a good many hundred yards of them, except once in the forest at Takahue, when one alighted near to us, but as soon as it became aware of our presence it was off like a shot from a gun.

On the Little Barrier Island this Parrakeet finds sanctuary and it is extremely common; in fact, I should think that the Parrot population of the Little Barrier is greater than that of the entire mainland. On first setting foot on that fascinating island the Parrakeets were the first birds which attracted attention. What a joy it was to see these brightly coloured birds only a few feet away instead of a quarter of a mile away as I had done on the mainland! Here they were utterly fearless, and my first "birdy", thrill after landing was to see one of these birds only a few feet away feeding on the seeds of the native flax which grew on the beach.

The favourite diet of the Parrakeets is the seeds of this plant
(*Phormium*), known locally as "flax", but bears no resemblance to
the plant known as flax in Europe. The seed pods are like small
hard bananas and are borne in clusters in a candelabra-like fashion
on stems which grow from 10 to 15 feet high. Each pod is packed
with peculiar flattened black seeds, the kernel of which in the
centre is white and nut-like to the taste. By the time the pods are
ripe one finds that nearly all have been torn to pieces by the
Parrakeets. On the Little Barrier I endeavoured to procure a
quantity of these seeds for my Norfolk Island Parrakeets, which
would also doubtless feed on them, since the plant is found on
Norfolk Island. As all the seeds were eaten as soon as they
ripened by the Parrakeets, I plucked a huge stock of the partly
ripe seed pods and placed them under bushes covered with
branches of trees, hoping that they would ripen in that way.
But on arriving at my treasure store some days later to collect the
seed I found that I had been outwitted by the Parrakeets, who had
discovered my hoard and systematically opened every pod.

Around the caretaker's house on the island the birds were comparatively tame, coming down to feed on the various seeds in the
garden and also on the apples which they seemed to relish in a half-
ripe state. It was when in the apple trees that we were able to
approach nearest to the birds, usually within two or three yards.

On a small group of islands which we visited we found the
Parrakeets very plentiful; on one of the very smallest islands they
were especially numerous. These islands are very small, and
although they were covered with the densest vegetation it was
amazing that they supported such a large Parrot population.
Most of the islands were almost inaccessible except the one where
the Parrakeets were so plentiful, and access to this was only gained
through climbing up a precipitous and partly dried-up waterfall.
During the rainy season it would be quite impossible to gain access
to this island at all. It is doubtless the inaccessibility of these
islands which has saved the Parrakeets.

The season had been very dry and there were only one or two
small pools on rocky ledges, and these formed the sole drinking
places for the birds on the island. All manner of native birds were
perfectly tame; the Parrakeets came round and settled within a
foot or two of one; in fact, they seemed to ignore the presence of
human beings, treating us as though we were non-existent. I have
seen few birds as tame in a wild state as the Parrakeets on this
island. A professional bird-catcher could have caught hundreds
in a morning. I spent two days and one night there, sleeping under
the shelter of a huge "flax" plant on the beach so that I could
observe the habits of the birds at their drinking places early in the
morning. In this I was disappointed, for I found that the best time
for seeing the Parrakeets was in the heat of the day, when there
was a constant stream of them coming to drink and bathe. It was
on this island that I heard for the first time the very distinctive
goat-like bleat of these birds which caused the Germans to call this
species "Ziegensittich". At first I thought there must be numerous
kinds in the "bush" as there are on many of the small islands off

the coast, but I soon found out the noise was made by the Parrakeets.

On the first three of the chain of islands which we visited the "flax" plants were entirely stripped of their seeds, and on these islands the Parrakeets were not nearly as plentiful as on the last island, where there was still a large quantity of seed, so it is obvious that the birds pass from one island to another as the supply of seeds runs short. There must be a considerable shortage of seed in the winter time, for I cannot think what the birds would eat except the hard seeds of a pampas-like grass called in the vernacular "toi-toi".

I spent a good many hours watching the Parrakeets at their drinking place and noticed that some of the birds seemed to prefer to settle on the perpendicular rocks and suck up the moisture which oozed through the cracks. I noted, too, that the birds were extremely agile in their movements on the rocks, running up perpendicular faces with the utmost ease.

On another fairly large island some miles away from the small group mentioned above we found the Parrakeets fairly numerous, but not nearly as tame as on the former islands. We were fortunate in finding a nest of almost fully fledged young ones within 2 feet of the ground. This nest was in a hollow puriri tree and the three youngsters could easily be reached by the hand. During the time my hand was inserted in the nest it got covered with tiny lice-like insects; when I withdrew it it was covered with a brown crawling mass of these creatures. Whether they came off the birds themselves or from the rotten wood I do not know, but it must certainly have been very uncomfortable for the birds. The youngsters were exact replicas of their parents except that the cere was very large, occupying quite half of the beak.

I understood from other naturalists that the Parrakeets were also very common on another small group of treeless islands to the north of New Zealand. These islands we intended to visit but did not do so. This was a matter of great regret to me, as I understood that owing to the absence of trees the birds were ground-nesting.

It is almost impossible to get hold of any of the Cyanoramphus Parrakeets now in New Zealand. On the mainland the birds are so scarce and wary that no one is able to catch them. Then there are no bird trappers, for all birds are protected and it is against the law to own any native birds except Keas and Zosterops. Even were it possible to get hold of any it would be impossible to get Government permission to export them out of the country.

All the islands I have mentioned are bird sanctuaries, where all bird-life is rigidly preserved and Government permission is needed to visit them. This is, of course, as it should be, for no one wants to think of the unique avifauna of New Zealand becoming extinct. But so long as the islands are protected the birds will be safe from extinction. The only fear now is from the increase of cats and rats upon the islands and from forest fires. It has been known for cruising parties to land on the islands and deliberately set fire to the forest during dry weather.

If the New Zealand Government paid as much attention to

the wicked and wanton burning of forests, with its terrible toll of bird life, which goes on everywhere unchecked, as it does to the slight moral lapses of some of its citizens it would earn the thanks of posterity.

Buller says, in writing of this species in the second edition of his work, published in 1888: "It is quite the cottagers' friend in New Zealand. Riding or driving through the suburbs of the provincial towns — Porirua and Karori districts, for example, near Wellington — you will notice in many of the farmers' houses and roadside cottages small wooden cages of primitive construction (often merely a candlebox or whisky-case, faced with wire-netting or thin bars) fixed up to the front of the building or under the simple verandah. On closer inspection each of these cages will be found to contain a tame Parrakeet — the pet of the rustic home and 'Pretty Poll' of the family. I have often been quite impressed at finding how attached these simple people become to their little captive." Now all is changed, for, search as I would from one end of the country to the other in my endeavour to obtain examples of this Parrakeet, I found only four examples in captivity, and these belonged to two naturalists who kept them and did not wish to part with them. Most New Zealanders do not know that a Parrakeet ever existed in their country, so rare is this bird to-day on the mainland.

THE YELLOW-FRONTED PARRAKEET (*Cyanorhamphus auriceps*)

Rare as the Red-fronted Parrakeet is, this bird is far rarer. It is almost unknown on the mainland of New Zealand, though in the middle of the last century it was even commoner than the other bird, appearing in flocks of countless numbers and devouring the corn and fruit of the settlers.

The first time we met with this rare bird in a state of freedom was on the Little Barrier Island. It will always stand out as one of the "red-letter" days of my life, for it was on that day we climbed Mount Archeria, the highest peak in the centre of the island. The island looked so sinister and foreboding as we approached it that I little dreamed of being able to stand on the top of its inaccessible-looking peak. But it proved easier than it looked. The climb was one of the most interesting I have ever done; up to 500 feet the way lay through dense manuka-bush, which is a secondary growth, replacing the burnt forest, after that the way lay through virgin forest of mixed growth until, at about 1,000 feet, this changed to kauri forest, there being many magnificent specimens of this giant forest tree. At about 2,000 feet this changed into semi-alpine rain-forest. Here it was a veritable fantastic fairyland, stranger than was ever pictured in the imagination of man. Everywhere seemed a fantastic mixture of trees, rocks, ferns, and mosses. In some places, strange as it may sound, it was like a fairy cavern where it was impossible to tell which was the ground, the rocks, or the trees. From the top it was possible to see the whole island, running in precipitous forest-covered ridges from the sea to the culminating point in the centre.

On the summit one stood in the clear rarified atmosphere in the brilliant sunshine, far above the rolling white mist clouds which the currents of air wove into strange wraith-like shapes. It was here that one realized the true significance of the beautiful Maori name "Hauturu", meaning "the resting place of the winds of Heaven".

It was at a height of about 2,000 feet that we first heard the chattering of Parrakeets, but it was a different note from that made by the Red-fronted, a softer and more melodious sound. I realized almost at once that it was the call of the Yellow-fronted Parrakeeet from the sound I had heard of a captive bird. But try as we would it was impossible to see the birds; the green of the plumage harmonized so well with that of the trees that in the dim light of the forest it was impossible to distinguish the birds. Fortunately on the way down, not far from the summit, a pair of Parrakeets flew down into a low sapling only a few feet away. One, to my surprise, proved to be a Yellow-fronted and the other a Red-fronted. It almost looked as though these were a pair, though this would be impossible. I watched the bird which I took to be the hen for about a quarter of an hour; she was quite tame and appeared to take quite as much interest in me as I took in her.

This delightful Parrakeet was at one time, fifty odd years ago, quite common in English aviaries, but has, alas! grown scarcer and scarcer until at last it is practically extinct in the North Island, the Little Barrier Island being one of the few places where it is found today, and even there it is far from common. This is strange, for it is supposed to be a very prolific breeder; Gutherie Smith records having found nine young ones in a nest.

The Yellow-fronted Parrakeet is now almost unknown in captivity in its native land, for apart from its rarity it is an offence against the law to keep it. I only came across two birds in my travels, both males, and I am quite sure these were the only ones in captivity. There is no more charming bird in existence from an aviculturist's point of view than this dainty and intelligent little Parrakeet. It is very beautiful, friendly, easy to feed, has no harsh notes, does not destroy woodwork, and is altogether the most delightful bird one could wish for. In the old days it was quite easily bred. It is a thousand pities that a small breeding stock could not be obtained so that the race could be perpetuated in captivity, but I am afraid that this will never be, and we must be thankful to think that this species still exists at all — it certainly would not have done had not certain islands been reserved as sanctuaries.

To show how misleading statements regarding birds may be, I heard whilst in the North Island that there was a large breeding colony of these birds in the forest country between Lake Waikaremoana and the Ruahine Mountains. I diligently traced down, from one to another, the original person who knew the whereabouts of the birds, only to find on reaching Lake Waikaremoana that the birds were plentiful — fifty years ago!

Buller says in his monumental work, *The Birds of New Zealand* "The Yellow-fronted Parrakeet is easily netted and when caged soon adapts itself to captivity. Twenty years ago a Mr Bills of Dunedin brought a hundred or more of them in cages to England, and they found ready purchasers at a guinea each." What would such a consignment be worth to-day?

I made a special trip down to Stewart Island, intending to visit some of the small outlying islands off the South Cape, mainly Mogg Island, Evening Island, and Hidden Island, where this Parrakeet is reported to be still found in considerable numbers. The Fates were against us. We set out in a 50ft. yacht, but the tempestuous seas proved too much for our small craft. For nearly a week we battled with the gales, having to seek, often enough, shelter in the wonderful inlets off the coast of Stewart Island. What a relief it used to be to find refuge in these quiet and beautiful waters which gave no indication of the fury outside! They were real havens of refuge, where we could light a fire and thaw our frozen limbs and get something to eat. Eventually, so bad did the seas become that we stood no earthly chance of ever arriving at our destination, so reluctantly we had to turn stern about and let the gale blow us back to safe anchorage in Half Moon Bay.

How these delicate-looking little Parrakeets manage to survive on these small islands, which for four or five months of the year are swept by bitter winds from the Antarctic, I do not know. The climate, by all account, resembles that of the West Coast of Scotland. But this bird, like so many others in New Zealand, seems to have been successful in adapting itself to its environment, for it is very evident that no member of the Parrot family could originally evolve under such adverse conditions.

I visited Ulva's Island in quest of this bird, but failed to find it, though I have no doubt that it was there, but our stays on the island were of very short duration and we had little time to make a thorough search of the dense forest.

Unlike the Red-fronted Parrakeet, this bird does not seem to find any of its food in the open, and I have never seen it on the flax plants. It seems, more or less, to feed upon the fruits of the forest trees.

Buller says: "At irregular periods after intervals of from seven to ten years this Parrakeet (in company with the preceding species) visits the settled and cultivated districts in astonishing numbers, swarming into the gardens and fields, devouring every kind of soft fruit, nibbling off the tender shoots on the orchard trees and eating up the pulse and grain in all directions. The last of these visitations occurred in the early part of 1886 and the one before that was at the close of 1877." Now all is changed, the Parrakeets have gone, never to return, and few are New Zealanders who have been fortunate enough to catch even a glimpse of this bird within recent years.

THE CHATHAM ISLAND PARRAKEET (Cyanorhamphus forbesi)

While the Red-fronted Parrakeet has many forms and subspecies found on far outlying islands, even as far as the Society Islands, the Yellow-fronted species has (or had) but one ally, namely Forbes or the Chatham Island Parrakeet. I should use the past tense for this bird has now joined the many species of the *Cyanorhamphus* group which have been exterminated by human agency. The extinction of this rare Parrakeet was directly brought about by a well-known ornithologist in this country, who years ago had agents in the Chathams collecting large series of skins of the various island species, many of which inhabited islands of only a few square miles. The Parrakeet soon disappeared and a party of scientists who had been over there recently failed to find it at all even though they made an extensive search. And all we have is a few perishable skins now transferred to America.

There are no records of the wild life of this bird so, like the Alpine Parrakeet, its history is now a closed book.

THE ALPINE PARRAKEET (Cyanorhamphus malherbei)

Try as I might, I was unable to trace anything about this dainty little Parrakeet. After travelling about in the various districts where it was found and by questioning many people who should have known it, I reluctantly came to the conclusion that if not actually on the verge of extinction it must be excessively rare. In the Southern Alps, its original habitat, it seemed to be quite unknown to anyone there. The only recent data concerning it was a fresh skin received at the Auckland Museum from the Nelson District. There is little doubt that in a few years' time this species will become extinct, for it is not found on any of the island sanctuaries, though it was reported to have been found on the Little Barrier Island and on the Hen Island. This was in the middle of the last century. It is certainly not found there now, though why it would become extinct, when its two congenitors are still found there, I do not know.

Buller in his *Birds of New Zealand* says of this bird, "In its native haunts in may be found frequenting the alpine scrub, in pairs or small parties, and is very tame and fearless. It is by no means uncommon in the wooded hills surrounding Nelson . . . At Nelson I saw many caged birds of this species, and one in particular was remarkable for the clear manner in which it articulated the words "Pretty Dick", repeating them all day long in the most untiring way."

Fifty or more years ago it was very occasionally imported into this country, but was never bred here, although there is a record of some young ones being reared in France in 1883. This unobtrusive little bird seems to have been known but for a few years, twenty or thirty at the most, and to have passed on, regretted only by those of us who deplore the wanton and wasteful destruction of Nature's most finished products. At the present rate another two or three hundred years will see the end of nearly all feathered life on this globe of ours, unless Man providentially manages, with the aid of poison gas, etc., to exterminate himself.

Looking through much literature I have been unable to find anything concerning this bird in captivity, and no one I met in New Zealand had either kept it or seen it alive, so its history now appears to be a closed book.

THE SOCIETY ISLAND PARRAKEET (Cyanorhamphus nealandicus)

Only three species of the *Cyanoramphus* Parrakeets were found in islands lying within the tropics and far from the typical habitat of this this group of birds. The Society Islands are a group of small and remote islands lying almost midway between Australia and South America. The species was first made known by Captain Cook, who first visited the island in the eighteenth century. Not long after the settling in the islands of the white traders the Parrakeet commenced to disappear and nearly fifty years ago it was reported as extinct, only two specimens being known. It was one of the few Parrakeets in this family which had a juvenile plumage.

The adult bird differed rather from most of the family. In colour, the forehead was black, a stripe through the eye and also the rump feathers being scarlet, the flight feathers blue and the rest of the body a bright green.

THE ULIETEA ISLAND PARRAKEET (Cyanorhamphus ulietanus)

Like the last-mentioned Parrakeet, this species is also extinct. It was confined to one small island in the Society Group and was reported extinct over a hundred years ago. This bird differed from all the other members of the family by having the plumage an olive brown colour, the head brownish black, the rump and basal upper tail coverts brownish red, the under parts olive yellow. It was the most distinctive in colouring of all the Cyanorhamphus Parrakeets. Nothing is known of its habits and only one or two skins are in existence.

THE LORD HOWE ISLAND PARRAKEET (Cyanorhamphus subflavinscens)

A Parrakeet very closely resembling the Norfolk Island Parrakeet (*Cyanorhamphus cooki*) was once plentiful on Lord Howe Island, but soon after the island was colonized by the white races the extermination of this Parrakeet began. It was shot, no doubt, by the settlers owing to its feeding upon the growing corn. This bird has now been extinct for between thirty and forty years. It was slightly smaller than *C. cooki*, but resembled it in colouring.

It is sad to think that of the fifteen known species of this family no less than six are now extinct and the others, with the exception of the Red-fronted Parrakeet which is only numerous on certain small islands, are on the verge of extinction.

THE KERMADEC ISLAND PARRAKEET (Cyanorhamphus n. cyanurus)

A matter of between five and six hundred miles to the north-east of New Zealand lie a group of small islands known as the Kermadecs, which until recent years were inhabited by a single family who raised sheep on one of the largest islands, namely Sunday Island. Finding that, with the slump in wool prices, farming on these lonely islands was not a commercial proposition, the family left and, I believe, the islands are now left to their original inhabitants, the birds.

Before the advent of man to this lonely spot a small Parrakeet of the *Cyanorhamphus* group was exceedingly plentiful, in fact it still is on some of the small outlying islands, where cats and rats have not been introduced. Where these pests have found a home on the larger islands the ranks of the Parrakeets have been sadly thinned out.

I had the good fortune whilst in New Zealand to see a true pair of these very rare Parrakeets, which were in the possession of a gentleman who had been on an expedition to the islands and had managed to secure this pair of birds. The hen was nesting, sitting I believe on eight eggs in a hollowed-out tree trunk in her small aviary. This, I understood, was the second time the birds had laid, the first time laying eight eggs which proved infertile. I left before the result of the second clutch was known. The birds were in rather cramped quarters and it was hardly to be wondered at that the eggs were infertile. The owner said he was going to re-wire a large aviary, occupied by Peafowl, with small mesh wire, so that the Parrakeets could be turned into it and thus have a better chance of breeding. It is to be hoped that this is done, for a brood of these rare birds would be a great acquisition from an aviculturist's point of view.

Though similar to the better known Red-fronted Parrakeet this bird differs in several points. It is larger, the wings and tail are a much brighter blue and the cheeks are a bright emerald green, also they struck me as being a different shape; for one thing the head appeared to be smaller and the neck much thicker. The red spot on the back is larger than in the Red-fronted, the hen can also be more easily told from the cock by her differently shaped head.

The owner of the birds, who, as previously mentioned had been to the Kermadecs, told me that the Parrakeets were very plentiful on the smaller islands but were very rare on Sunday Island – the one where the sheep farm had been. They nested in crevices in the ground and fed mainly on grass seed.

The birds referred to were in very fine condition, being fed mainly on natural food with little seed, the hen of the pair was not the original one, she having died of egg binding after laying twenty eggs.

A pair of these birds were imported into this country a few years ago, having been presented to the late Governor who, when he retired, brought them back to Great Britain, and for all I know they may still be here.

If this chapter happens to meet with the eye of the owner of the birds in New Zealand perhaps he will be good enough to send us a little more information about them, which I am sure would be very welcome, as so little seems to be known of these exceedingly rare birds.

There is only one skin of this bird in the British Museum and that was obtained from Raoul Island.

BREEDING RECOMMENCED

In the mid-1930s breeding of the Yellow Fronted Parrakeet was restarted. Without that action being taken there is little doubt that members of the genus would have been lost. The instigator appears to have been the doyen of foreign bird enthusiasts E.J. Boosey who, with his partner, ran the Keston Foreign Bird Farm. He recorded his experiences in *The Foreigner* a bi-monthly magazine issued by his company.

Much of what he states applies equally today and therefore an edited version is reproduced below:

HOW TO BREED THE YELLOW-FRONTED NEW ZEALAND PARRAKEET (Cyanoramphus auriceps)

Owing to their rarity and the strict laws that prohibit their export from New Zealand and the neighbouring islands, the *Cyanoramphus* Parrakeets are nowadays practically unknown to aviculture.

Many years ago, one member of the genus — the Red-fronted New Zealand — seems to have been fairly extensively kept and to have had the reputation of being an extremely prolific breeder.

Cyanoramphus auriceps, the subject of this article, is now probably the rarest of the family and shares with the Alpine Parrakeet, *C. malherbi,* the distinction of being the smallest member of the whole group, being only 9.6inches long or about the size of a Bourke's or a Blue-winged Grass Parrakeet.

Their prevailing colour is a rich, rather dark moss-green paler on the breast, a band above the beak and a patch on the flanks bright red, fore-part of the crown golden-yellow; some blue on the lower edge of the wings; bill a pretty silver, shading to black at the tip. The eyes are very striking, owing to their brilliant ruby red irides.

One great advantage they possess is the ease with which they may be sexed, the hens being not only less brightly coloured, but a good two sizes smaller than their mates, so that it is quite possible to tell them apart at a glance even from some distance away. So marked is this distinction that it reminds one more of the difference existing between the size of the sexes of certain of the Raptorials, such as the Sparrow-hawk, though in their case, of course, it is the hen who is the larger.

Though, as will be seen, they are by no means gaudily coloured, yet I think their really remarkable tameness, intelligence, and vivacity would cause anyone who had ever been lucky enough to possess a pair, to rank them very high indeed on their list of favourites. If someone suddenly hit upon the bright idea of holding a *concours d'elegance* of Parrakeets, and if, furthermore, I happened to be the individual chosen for the invidious task of placing the entrants in their order of merit, I should, at any rate, have one compensation — the awarding of the first prize would be easy. I should give it without hesitation to the Princess of Wales', that rare and lovely Parrakeet from Australia which nature has seen fit to endow with what one cannot help thinking is a good deal more than its fair share of beauty of form and charm of disposition. But the awarding of the second prize would be more difficult; yet, if general attractiveness of character and intelligence ranked high and brilliance of plumage were a secondary consideration, I think I know on which of two birds my choice would fall. It would be either Bourke's Parrakeet or the subject of this article.

If Yellow-fronted New Zealands will not, as does a Princess of Wales', greet one with shrill screams of delight as soon as one goes near their aviary, they will nevertheless become even more lively than usual, just to show you how pleased they are to see you. When you get quite close to their aviary, they will hop on to the wire netting, perhaps rather high up, and then — a thing which few other Parrakeets ever do — they will run rapidly *downwards* until on a level with your face. They then subject you to a careful bright-eyed scrutiny, after which they will probably fly down on to the ground, the whole manoeuvre being typical of all their actions, which I think are best described as a "hop, skip and a jump."

Once on terra firma they execute several long jumps, varied with short hops, after which they settle down to a minute examination of the earthen floor of their flight. This process is most amusing, and I shouldn't like to say how many precious hours I've wasted, watching them.

First of all, the pair will walk about side by side, scratching in the soil occasionally with their long legs after the manner of poultry.[1] (Incidentally, no other group of Parrakeets have this purely gallinaceous habit). Then one of them, perhaps the cock, will come across what he considers to be a particularly intriguing stone or small lump of earth. Instantly, his mate will rush up to him to be, as it were, "in at the kill"; but he usually has other ideas on the subject, and all she gets is a firm, yet gentle, push in the face from her husband's out-stretched foot, and she generally takes the hint and goes off prospecting on her own.

Left to himself, her husband examines his find at his leisure. First of all, it is pushed aside to see if anything of interest lies beneath it; then, in one foot — though he uses if far more as if it were a hand — he will pick up the object of his interest — be it a leaf or a stone or merely a piece of earth — and turning it first this way, then that, subject it to the most careful examination.

Sometimes this takes a considerable time, but usually he is able to decide at once that it is unworthy of further attention, and throwing it aside, goes off after his wife, who being similarly employed, dismisses her husband with as little ceremony as he had employed to her, namely a determined push in the face.

Soon after this, both will fly up into their aviary, after which a bout of extreme activity ensues, both of them hopping, flying and jumping so quickly that their separate movements are difficult to follow.

I have devoted more space than usual to a description of the birds' actions and general behaviour in an aviary, because it is in these, and in their curious voices that all the *Cyanoramphus*

Parrakeets differ so utterly from any other group. When one first hears their cry, one imagines a small Parrakeet to be the very last possible source from which it could have emanated. It is, in fact, exactly like the bleating of a sheep heard from some distance away. However unattractive and monotonous this may sound in print, it is entirely saved from being either through the bird's habit of varying the tone and *tempo* to suit its moods.

Sometimes it is rather slow and grave. At others it sounds light-hearted and gay, being higher-pitched and much more quickly reiterated. Then again, there is an intermediate, slightly absent-minded, meditative note which they often employ when engaging in their absorbing pastime of treasure-hunting, which I have already described.

Cock *Cyanoramphus* Parrakeets are reputed to be liable to murder their wives at any moment, and without the slightest provocation. Personally, I am inclined to doubt this, and it certainly does not apply to the Yellow-fronted, though it may to some of the larger members of the genus, such as the Norfolk Island, which has a much more powerful beak.[2]

Yellow-fronts are very willing to go to nest, and hens are quite easily suited with a nest box. The six young ones bred here at Keston last season from one pair were reared in a wooden box, with a hole near the top, about 18ins. deep by 7ins. square, containing a few inches of earth on top of which an inverted square of turf had been placed, the box being hung vertically under slight over-head shelter in the open flight.[3]

It was rather late in the season, when by a stroke of luck we were able to obtain a proper husband for the hen, who had originally, as a make-shift, been mated in April to a cock Blue-wing their four eggs proving unfertile. When introduced to the cock Yellow-front, however, she immediately went to nest again, laying a clutch of six eggs, all of which were successfully hatched and reared.

During all this time she was left severely alone and we were only made aware that a brood had hatched by the curious cry of the young ones being fed in the nest, which is just as distinctive as their parents sheep-like bleating, and resembles nothing so much as the far-off, high-pitched screaming of swifts as they wheel in wide circles on a summer evening.

Yellow-fronts are not difficult to feed, but they need careful rationing, particularly of such oily seeds as hemp and sunflower. Their staple seed mixture should consist of one part canary, one part white millet, quarter part brown millet, quarter part oats, with a very small pinch of hemp, and not more than a dozen grains of sunflower per day to each bird. The latter seed, particularly seems in any considerable quantity to upset their digestions. They should be given a continuous supply of millet spray and fresh sweet apples, not only when they have young ones to feed, but the whole year round.

When they have a brood to cater for, a few handfuls of their ordinary seed should be thrown daily to sprout on a mound of earth, or preferably peat-moss, in the open flight. The amounts of hemp and sunflower can both be gradually increased until, just before the young ones are due to leave the nest, the parents are being given two handfuls of sunflower and one of hemp thrown on their mound morning and evening, in addition to canary and oats and millet.

At all times they are great green-food eaters, and particularly appreciate a freshly-cut square of turf, which is a useful way of providing them with green food during the winter months. Not only will they eat the grass, but tear the turf to pieces, eating the root as well.

During the breeding season they should be given, besides turf, as many spinach-beet leaves as they will eat. A Mr. Bouskill, who reared them about forty years ago, and who seems, besides ourselves, to have been the only other aviculturist ever to have bred the Yellow-fronted New Zealand in England, recommends numerous mealworms as part of their diet; of this I can only say that none of those we have here will touch them. This, however, is probably only another of those cases one so often encounters of individual preference among birds of the same species, and I should certainly imagine that mealworms, in moderation, would be a wholesome addition to their diet if they could be induced to take them.

Yellow-fronts have only one real failing as aviary birds, and that is they cannot be considered entirely hardy.[4] This is the more extraordinary as their native climate is anything but genial, since, at any rate in winter, they have to put up with high winds and a decidedly lower temperature, in addition to frequent fogs. Yet,

---

FOOTNOTE:

*Comments on Mr Boosey's Contribution:

1. This trait has been observed by one or two breeders and certainly appears to be in accordance with the natural behaviour of birds in the wild (see Mr Porter's comments early in this chapter) but the author has found that some birds in captivity do not scratch. Possibly the fashion to provide concrete floors in aviaries has eliminated the urge in some species. My own birds scratch constantly.

2. The experience of non-aggressiveness has been recorded by many breeders. Through careful selection over many years the unpleasant trait may have been bred out. Sydney Porter (*ibid*) states how friendly and tame they are in the wild and this is still the same in captivity. However, as all experienced bird fanciers know birds which are friendly and extrovert can turn and become quite vicious, particularly in the breeding season. Our experience tends to suggest that generally Kakarikis are free from vice.

3. Selection of the most appropriate nest boxes is very important. If too small chicks are squashed and, if too large, eggs get scattered.

4. Again opinions differ. Many breeders regard Kakirikis as being quite hardy. It would appear though that 50 years on they are more hardy than indicated by Mr Boosey. Nevertheless, for those with a bird house an internal flight may be an advantage for those winter months when frost and snow prevail.

in this country, they are far more susceptible to our unpleasant winter weather — which incidentally must be so very like their own — than, for example, the Hooded Parrakeet, which hails from tropical northern Australia, yet will winter out of doors in an unheated aviary without so much as turning a hair, however bitter the weather may be.

Judging by our experience, therefore, Yellow-fronts are far best kept in a roomy flight-cage in a warm bird-room from the beginning of October to the middle of April.

MORE RECENT VIEWS

More recent findings on *Cyanoramphus* are now summarised. For more detailed information readers are referred to *The Parrots of the World*, Joseph M. Forshaw, 1972 and subsequent editions:

1. **Red-Fronted Parrakeets** (8 sub-species). These are now rare birds, but can be found on the outer islands such as Little Barrier Island, Auckland Islands and Antipodes Island.

2. **Yellow-Fronted Parrakeets** (2 sub-species). After a positive falling off in numbers they are mutliplying in the forest regions. Forshaw suggests they are tree-dwellers to a greater extent than the Red-Fronted Parrakeets which tend to rely on ground cover.

3. **Orange-Fronted Parrakeet**. This Parrakeet continues to be very rare and as a result very little is known of its habits or feeding details. Apparently it has been sighted on rare occasions, the last recording being about 20 years ago.

Forshaw suggests an orange frontal band for this bird, but the painting by W.T. Cooper in *The Parrots of the World* shows what could be a crimson band (possibly reddy-orange), very little different from the Yellow-Fronted Parrakett shown on the same illustration. This anomally is commented on by the author in the descriptions of the birds in Chapter 3. Unfortunately, because of the rarity of the Orange-Fronted Parrakeet, there is no way of checking whether the frontal area of the head should be red or orange.

Significantly the Yellow-Fronted Parrakeet has a red

frontal band and, therefore, it would appear that the
illustration by Cooper is correct. Presumably the original
genus had a red frontal area and the other two are
variations. Possibly the Red-Fronted Parrakeet is the
nominate race and the other two are mutations. There is
no evidence to support this statement, but if seems more
likely for colours to come lighter than to come darker. The
experience of the author in colour breeding with various
birds has been that darker colours are more difficult to
maintain, whereas pigmentation losses tend to occur fairly
easily.

THE PRESENT POSITION

Over the years breeding has continued so that Red-
Yellow-and Orange Fronted Kakarikis are available. There
are well-founded grounds for suggesting that purity of blood
and colour are open to doubt. Hybrids have been produced
which are not strictly in accordance with the descriptions
of species found in the wild.

The fact remains that these delightful birds have been
snatched back from extinction and we are now able to
enjoy their companionship.

FOOTNOTE – NORFOLK ISLAND PARRAKEET. As this book goes to
press news comes in that *Cyanoramphus n. Cooki* has been bred in captivity on
Norfolk Island by staff of the Australian National Parks and Wildlife Services,
reported by Mr John Hicks. As Mr I.S. Dyer reports, this is a major achieve-
ment in captive breeding (*The Parrot Society Magazine*, April 1989).

Fig 2-2 Typical New Zealand Bush. Note: Many of the smaller islands
support little or no vegetation (see earlier text)

NEW ZEALAND
PARRAKEETS
IN
AVICULTURE

THE GOLDEN HEADED PARROT OF NEW ZEALAND
(Cyanoramphus Auriceps)

It was an exceedingly pretty, inoffensive little creature, green as to its general colour, but with a narrow band of red on its forehead, succeeded by a wider one of a golden yellow that reached to the middle of the top of the head. The eyes were reddish-brown, and the bill pale lead-colour; the long tarsi and the toes were bluish-slate-grey. The breast and the rest of the under parts were yellowish-green and the shoulders blue.

Dr. W. T. Green (*ibid*) describing a bird he had acquired in the 1890's. Note the earlier name for the Yellow-Fronted New Zealand Parrakeet.

Fig. 3-1 Head Study of Red-Fronted Kakariki. Note the side patch which appears only on this species and not on the Yellow or Orange Fronted (Photo: Susan Lawson)

CHAPTER 3
NEW ZEALAND PARRAKEETS IN AVICULTURE

DISTRIBUTION

These distinctive parrakeets originate from New Zealand and the surrounding small islands where in Victorian times they were regarded as a social and economic menace creating havoc rather like a plague of locusts. The farmers reacted violently and, as a result, they were exterminated in large quantities.

The Red-fronted Parrakeet is now a protected species in New Zealand.

Some of these birds live quite near to the South Pole, so obviously they are quite hardy. In any event they breed quite easily in captivity so for all practical purposes they are fully domesticated in the UK and other countries. (See Distribution Map, Fig.2-1)

ORIGIN OF NAME

In popular usage for some time now the description **Kakariki** is generally accepted for a generic term to identify these parrakeets. How the name originated is not always understood. Two versions are given by different writers:

(a) From the sound of their cry; kiki
(b) Based on the Maori language, simply meaning a small parrot.

The latter interpretation probably represents the more acceptable meaning.

TEMPERAMENT WITH OTHER BIRDS

Most breeders of Kakarikis* suggest that they are of equable temperament being friendly and agreeable with other species. This has been our experience.

Breeders in the past have had problems, usually a "rogue" cock who kills his wife and others who are introduced into the aviary. This behaviour is recorded by the Marquess of Tavistock (*Parrots and Parrot-Like Birds*) who cites the birds kept by a Canon Dutton not only killed their companions but also ate them!

The fact remains that like many other species of Parrakeet — especially at breeding times — they do tend to be aggressive and have to be watched.

If in doubt with a particular cock or hen it is wise to clip *one* wing, thus rendering him less mobile. Any other birds can then escape. However, this is a step which is best avoided because it spoils the birds and reduces the enjoyment of seeing them fly around.

In any event follow the normal practice of keeping one pair of Kakarikis only in an aviary and this reduces the chance of conflict.

These will normally be quite agreeable to other types of birds in the aviary. The author has kept doves, budgerigars and even cockatiels with Kakarikis without problem.

The conclusion must be that usually Kakarikis are agreeable together and quite friendly with other genera and care should be taken to ensure that harmony prevails.

WITH BIRD-KEEPERS

Kakarikis are friendly characters who become quite docile.

If watched through the aviary wire they will come quite close and are very tame. They run up the wire or up the sides of the aviary and generally behave in ways which are quite different from that displayed by other Parrakeets, being constantly on the move. They will run along a ledge and then fly to a perch and back again.

There is no set pattern to their behaviour and this makes

---

*The plural may be spelt as "Kakariki", "Kakarikies", or as adopted in this book.

them very interesting to watch.

If a dark corner or ledge is available they will perch there. The author has an overhanging roof and the kakarikis insist on going to roost in the dark recess even though perches and parts of bushes are available for perching. The Budgerigars in the same aviary keep to the conventional roosting places.

When attending to chores in the bird-room there is no panic from the Kakarikis. They will fly around, but not with the wildness found with some types of birds. They are even tamer than their aviary companions, the Budgerigars.

They are not known for their talking abilities but they can be taught and this adds to their interest as aviary birds.

Unusually for Parrakeets, they do not chew everything in sight.

CONCLUSION

Kakirikis have much to recommend them on the following grounds:

1. Colourful
2. Apparently intelligent and inquisitive and they appear to like domesticity
3. Lively and unpredictable in behaviour
4. Generally live in harmony
5. Fairly easy to breed (see Chapter 7)*
6. Require standard Parrakeet-type foods which present no problems
7. Do not destroy wooden nest boxes and aviaries

Accordingly they can be recommended as ideal birds for the aviary where they will give many hours of enjoyment to the bird keeper.

Against them is the occasional problem from a rebel cock bird when he has to be watched. This does not seem wide spread.

In addition some breeders have alleged a relative short life in an aviary.

*The experiences of at least two breeders suggest that Kakarikis prefer an aviary and as little disturbance as possible or eggs may be neglected or broken. (See Parrot Society Magazine Vol.XII, No.11, Nov.1978, where W. Hardy relates his experiences when keeping Kakarikis in a large wooden cage. The five eggs were broken by the birds.

This is not a general finding so there must be a reason for some failures; this may be incorrect feeding, over exposure to the weather resulting in chills, or bad management. They must have adequate space for flying and a covered shed for relaxing in and they should then retain their health and vitality for many years.

THE SPECIES EXPLAINED

There is some difficulty in giving precise descriptions of the main species, which are very similar. The distinguishing features are connected with the head:

a) Brow band (deep crimson red or reddish-orange)

b) Upper head band (red, yellow or orange)

It is the colour of these two which determines the precise species although, in practice they have been interbred to such an extent that they may be difficult to find in their exactly pure form. However, this should not be exaggerated because the author has visited different bird fanciers and seen Red-Fronted Parrakeets as well as Yellows.

According to I.S. Dyer (*Kakariki*) many of the so called Orange and Yellow Fronted Kakarikis are hybrids and possess a patch behind the eyes which should be on the Red Fronted Species only.*

In fact, it seems likely from the experiences of the different breeders that the modern Orange Fronted birds are really crosses, possibly from the Yellows and Reds.

DESCRIPTIONS

NEW ZEALAND PARRAKEETS OR KAKARIKIS

1. Red Fronted Parrakeets
2. Yellow Fronted Parrakeets
3. Orange Fronted Parrakeets
4. Cinnamon (a new colour mutation)

*Readers are referred to the Magazine of the Parrot Society for January and February 1989 for a feature by G. Carss and a reply by Mr I.S. Dyer on the dangers of cross-breeding the different colours.

Fig. 3-2 Head and Rump Markings of Red Fronted Kakarikis
Note: Red colour is a bright crimson red

The **Red Fronted** are known as *Cyanoramphus novaezelandiae* and there are supposed to be nine races, although the bird keeper need not worry too much about that fact. In the wild many races have disappeared altogether so obviously the aviculturist must view those in existence as being of importance.

The fact that races or sub-species existed and may still exist can be of considerable interest to the ornithologist but there is no way of distinguishing captive stock as being one race or another this being dependent on the original source of other species.

The **Yellow Fronted** (two sub-species) come under the same name *Cyanoramphus*, but with the addition of *auriceps* to show the variation.

As stated earlier they are part of the Parrot Family known as *Psittacinae*. The name of the race *Cyanoramphus* refers to the bill or beak which is cyan; ie, Blue. In fact the beak is a grey-blue with a black tip, but when the sunlight shines on it, different colours may be seen, sometimes almost like mother-of-pearl.

The **Orange Fronted** is known as *Cyanoramphus Malherbi* and may exist in New Zealand, but is rarely seen in captivity, although hybrids may appear to be this species.

OTHER DETAILS

Size: Around 10 inches long (25cm) to about 12 inches (30cm)

The Yellow and Orange Fronted tend to be at least 1inch smaller. In all species the females are smaller than the matching male, again by 1 inch (2.54cm) or a little more.

The Kakariki is a medium sized bird with no exaggerated features. Unlike many other parrots the head does not appear large and there is very little indentation between the back of the head and the shoulders; ie, the neck.

The tail is quite long and when viewed sideways appears to represent about half the overall length.

As noted, females are smaller in length; they also tend to have smaller heads and beaks.

Colour: Body, Rich darkish green with an intermingling of yellow on some species. The Red Fronted is usually regarded as being darker in colour with less yellow, but many Yellow Fronted are also quite dark in the body.

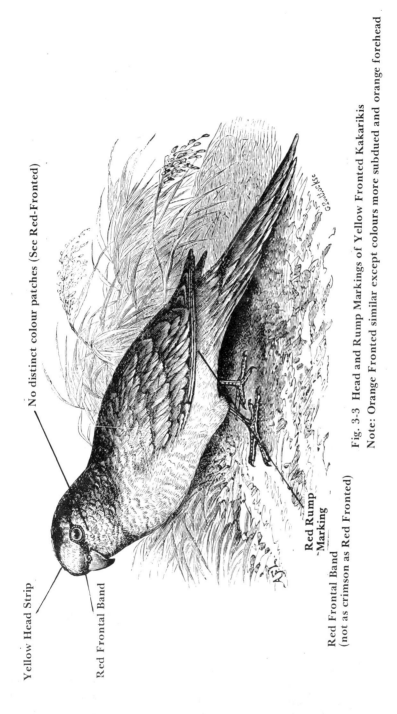

No distinct colour patches (See Red-Fronted)

Yellow Head Strip

Red Frontal Band

Red Frontal Band
(not as crimson as Red Fronted)

Red Rump
Marking

Fig. 3-3 Head and Rump Markings of Yellow Fronted Kakarikis
Note: Orange Fronted similar except colours more subdued and orange forehead

Rump: red patches at side

Wings: rich dark blue on the wings viewed when the bird is perched, ie on the outer flight feathers.

Tail: Broad and swallow-shaped and of a vivid grass green colour with a tinging of yellow and dark shading on some parts.

Head: Since the head determines the species it follows that great attention should be paid to this aspect.

> The brow is red in both Yellow-Fronted and Red-Fronted birds with an orange colour in Orange-Fronted Kakarikis. It will be noted that the Yellow-Fronted Parrakeet has a reddish brow yet logically this should be yellow.
> In the Orange-Fronted the brow is a bright orange or reddish-orange and the skull is a yellowish colour. A similar colour exists for the Yellow-Fronted Kakarikis although many descriptions specify that the upper head should be an orange colour.

Red-Fronted Side Bands
    The Red-Fronted Parrakeets have distinct side pieces extending from the base of the beak to behind the eye and it is the latter patch which is found only in pure Red species including related species such as *Cyanoramphus cooki* (see illustration).

Eyes: The overall impression of the eyes is dark brown with a bright red iris. They are full of expression and alertness.

Legs: The legs are a browny colour and appear slender and long, except when the Kakariki is walking or sitting when they will be hidden by the plentiful feathering which is a characteristic of the genus.

SPECIAL NOTE ON OTHER COLOURS
Whether a colour should really be recognised as a mutation from a single breeding is a doubtful point. Strictly speaking a true mutation should be capable of reproducing itself or it is simply an

"off colour "a term recognised in poultry breeding for many years.

Colours which are likely to become established in the forsee-able future are:

1. **Cinnamon**   2. **Pied**
3. **Lutino**   4. **Blue**

Experience has shown that these colours will be bred from green birds (c f. Ringnecks). Once a Blue is available Whites should be possible. At present Cinnamon and a form of Pied (parti – coloured)are available, but these have to be improved before they can be said to be established colours.

OTHER SPECIES – CYANORPHAMPUS*

Three other species have also been known:

1. C.COOKI (Norfolk Island Parrakeet)
This genus breeds on the ground and Norfolk Island where it existed was infested with rats. Accordingly, many years ago it was in danger of becoming extinct. The exact position at present is obscure. It is larger than the nominate form of Kakariki. Those in captivity do breed, and recently they have been bred on Norfolk Island for release into the wild.

2. C. UNICOLOR (Antipodes Island Green Parrakeet)
This is self-green and at 13ins is larger than the Continental New Zealand Parrakeets (Kakarikis). There is no record of successful keeping in aviaries, but many years ago it was at the London Zoo.

3. C.SAISSETI (Saisset's Parrakeet)
This rare and possibly extinct Parrakeet was found in New Caledonia. Around 12.6 inches long it was at the London Zoo, but may now have disappeared.

*The reader is also referred to Chapter 1, the notes from the writing of Sydney Porter, where other extinct species are commented on.

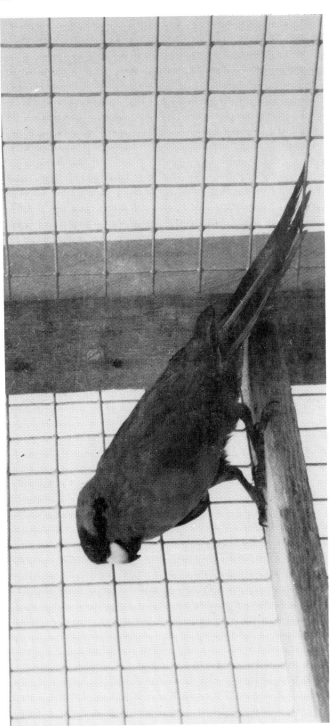

Fig. 3·4   A Red-Fronted Kakariki in a modern aviary (Photo: Susan Lawson)

4
ACCOMMODATION

Fig. 4-1 A Parrot Cage
(not recommended for Kakarikis)

Fig. 4-2 An Indoor Flight (just adequate but doubtful for breeding)

CHAPTER 4

KEEPING KAKARIKIS

ADEQUATE SPACE ESSENTIAL

Kakarikis may be kept in cages or aviaries, but, if the former, it is usually stressed that the cages should be as large as possible so that the birds can exercise. They are constantly on the move and to limit them within small cages appears rather cruel. Filled with curiosity in any aviary, the Kakarikis run or fly from one part to another, constantly exploring so very restricted space will simply not suffice.

The habit of feeding on the ground and even scratching like poultry is a habit to be considered and obviously cages cannot provide the necessary conditions for their natural habits.

With all birds in captivity the aim should be to make the environment as near as possible to natural conditions. Kakarikis come from remote areas, feeding on berries and insects and nesting in hollow trees or rocks. What could be more unnatural than a cage!

LIFE IN CAPTIVITY

The appropriate conditions; ie, adequate space and fresh air with protection from the inclement weather and predators are vital for keeping and breeding Kakarikis. An aviary is usually essential, covered in wire mesh.

Wire Mesh
Parrots and Parrot-like birds require fairly strong netting which may be:
1. Conventional wire-netting
2. Weld mesh which has perfectly joined squares or rectangles giving a neat appearance.

There is a tendency to use weld mesh these days although in fact·wire netting is quite adequate and may be cheaper. The thickness should be appropriate for the birds being kept, thus:

Parrakeets (including Kakarikis)
½ x ½ inch (12mm) 16 wire guage thick

Parrots
1 inch x 1 inch (25mm) and 12 guage thick.

Remember it is also desirable to keep wild birds out of the aviary so a small size is preferable, but note the cost rises dramatically when the smaller sizes are used.

GENERAL PRINCIPLES

Housing Parrots and Parrakeets in **appropriate** cages or aviaries is of vital importance to their health and well-being. If breeding is to be attempted, conditions must be excellent or efforts will be wasted.

The fancier's choice will be influenced by what he can afford. Some modern breeders are prepared to sacrifice a great deal to build a purpose-made aviary of brick with windows and ventiliation. In the long run such expenditure may well be justified, but many fanciers manage very well with home made sheds and flights.

Cages may serve many purposes – housing, breeding, showing, or training. They may be kept in a room in a dwelling house for the pet bird or in a bird room specially made for the purpose. The use of small open cages has long been the subject of criticism; they are only suitable where there are no draughts.

There is now legal recognition that birds should not be kept in small show-type cages for long periods. They are too restricting and, therefore, not recommended for a permanent home. Obviously a cage-bird like a parrot should have a very large cage.

Cages
The types of cages found in use are as follows:

1. Domestic Fancy Cages for use in the home.
These are usually pleasing in design and hang on

stands or rest on a small table. For the enthusiast with money to spend on antiques there are some splendid cages which will do justice to the most discerning householder. However, they can be very generous in space with many compartments. For parrots, very strong cages are essential with thick wire.

2. Breeding Cages which may have one or more compartments — single, double or treble.
Basically they are wooden boxes with wire fronts. They enable the birds to have privacy. Usually the smaller type are unsuitable for parrots which would be restricted and chew through the wood.

3. Small Indoor Flights.

4. Nursery Cages for rearing youngsters when feather pecking and bullying takes place. This would not apply if birds are kept in aviaries.

5. Show Cages which may be the **open wire type** or **box cages**. The specialist clubs lay down the precise cage to be used for each breed and these must be used in accordance with the regulations of the particular club. The statutory requirements are laid down by the various acts in existence in the UK and in other countries.

Aviaries

The design of the aviary is of great importance and therefore time should be taken to make sure the best structure possible is made or obtained. This can be attractive as well as functional and, in a garden, landscaping is very appropriate. Lawns, bushes, rustic fences, trellis work and other gardening features all help to create the correct environment.

FUNCTIONAL REQUIREMENTS

Factors to consider when designing an aviary are as follows:

1. Size of house or sleeping shed
2. Flights including covered section

3. Insulation and ventilation
4. Lighting
5. Protection from disease and predators
6. Perches and related equipment
7. Safety porches
8. Landscaping and Aesthetic Requirements

The functional requirements cover the essentials for sound management and good health. These can be achieved in a solid building made of corrugated tin, but the impression can be one of make-shift economy which is possibly fine for a smallholding, but not for beautiful birds in a garden.

Both wooden and metal structures may be purchased which are pleasing in design. They can be adapted with internal partitions as well as being insulated.

Larger buildings are available in the form of stables or dog kennels and, again, they may be adapted for breeding rooms or indoor aviaries. They are usually of very solid construction and whilst costly they lend themselves to modification without difficulty. They are likely to suit the breeder who wishes to keep and breed a considerable number of birds.

SIZE OF AVIARIES

There is no hard and fast rule on the optimum size aviary. Usually, though, a minimum size of floor space of 1 square foot (30cm) per bird is taken as a guide (with the larger parrots requiring twice as much), but to allow for breeding around 1 square metre per bird is desirable. At the end of each season the space should be reviewed for young birds hatched can soon cause overcrowding.

A view often expressed is that *cubic* capacity should not be taken as a guide to the size of aviary required. Whilst this may be the case it is also true that the extent of the flights attached to aviaries will be important in determining whether birds have adequate room. If they are flying around or perching on the flights they will be relieving pressure on the aviary proper (the sleeping apartment).

CONSTRUCTION

Today there are many excellent sheds available from the local garden and bird centres. There are also many very

Fig. 4·3 Block of Aviaries for housing pairs of Kakarikis. Originally designed for Lovebirds, but suitable for all small Parrakeets

poor structures. Very thin board affixed with wire staples will not last; nor will it give adequate protection to the birds. Avoid such sheds because in the long run the apparent cheapness will prove to be very expensive.

Essentials are as follows:

1. Solid timber preferably lined with some form of insulating board (not soft material which the birds can peck away). Tongue and grooved boarding is very desirable because this avoids draughts. Usually ¾inch board (around 30mm) is recommended.

2. The roof should be watertight and easily maintained (a coat of tar and creosote each year should keep it in good order). Perspex sheets give adequate light, but tend to be cold in winter and hot in summer, although they are acceptable for the covered flight which has wire netting on the outside. Boards and roofing felt are probably the best method for keeping the shed dry, but remember that adequate lighting is still essential within the shed.

3. Windows and entrance holes should be provided for adequate light and exits (which also give some ventilation).
Windows should be made so they can be opened, but without draughts, and properly wire netted so that the birds cannot escape through openings. In addition, shutters or circular outlets fitted to the sides may be used for:

a) ventilation;
or
b) allowing birds to fly through the openings into the outdoor flights (it may be desirable to close these in winter)

4. The floor should be made of wood (above the ground) or concrete. Thick timber, well supported is essential or rats, mice and other vermin will find their way in. Moreover, if not raised above the earth the wood will rot and after a few years will let in damp and cold. Concrete is obviously the answer, but this tends to be

cold so a good covering of clean wood shavings is essential (renewed when it becomes soiled). Alternatively, a shed with a wooden floor can be placed on concrete or flagstones.

The Bird Room

Aviary and Bird-Room tend to be descriptions of the same thing. However, some people prefer to refer to a bird-room as a specially fitted building, or a room within a building, where all essentials can be kept and the birds can be housed in considerable comfort. Certainly for successful all-the-year-round management well-built insulated accommodation is vital.

An aviary purchased from a garden centre will probably have all the essentials for keeping a few birds, but it will not provide them with all their needs for successful breeding and showing.

If space permits an aviary and bird-room may be advisable, thus allowing birds to be kept in comfort at all times as well as providing the means for training for shows. Taken to the ultimate there should also be provision for running water indoors and electricity for light and heat.

INSULATION AND VENTILATION

The aviary or bird-room should be insulated so as to avoid extremes in temperature. If a brick building is used then a wooden frame can be built into the structure with some form of cavity and the inner skin would be plaster board, hard board or one of the many special boards now available. Polystyrene tiles are not suitable because they tend to flake and are a fire hazard. However, some manufacturers have produced special insulating materials for commercial poultry sheds and these could well be worth investigating. Remember though that unless protected with wire netting some parrots will chew all in sight.

VENTILATION

The provision of adequate air without excessive draughts should receive attention. This question is also linked with the provision of windows, which may be allowed to open with metal gauze or wire netting to cover the opening. Small holes drilled in the side of the shed will also provide ventilation as will some form of grille arrangement which will open and close.

Ideally the inlet for air should be towards the top of the building. When the air enters it sinks to the ground and, when warmed up, will rise and may be let out at roof level. If the inlet opening is too near the bottom of the building the inrush of air will be too fierce and will cause discomfort.

The aim should be to get the air to circulate so as to remove any foul air or gases, but not to make the aviary too cold. Accordingly, the outside temperature should be considered and in the summer months wire netting covered openings could be beneficial. In winter a different story emerges because the conservation of heat is important, even if there is some loss of ventilation in the bird-room proper (ie, sleeping quarters). Except on very bad days (cold or wet) the birds should always be allowed access to a flight and thereby breathe a plentiful supply of fresh air.

Some breeders never use any heat in a bird-room, whereas others insist that no results are possible without the means of keeping the temperature at not less than around 50°F. Certainly for making an early start with breeding and to make sure that water does not freeze some form of heating is advisable.

In modern times the tendency is to employ tubular heaters which are totally enclosed and use a small amount of electricity. A typical heater is shown opposite; it is usually supplied in convenient lengths of around 1 metre upwards and can be fitted easily and requires no maintenance. Because of its lower power consumption it may be operated without a thermostat, simply being turned off when the weather is mild.

The position of the aviary also affects heat and light. The author has an aviary at the side of a large lawn with hedges on one side and a wire netting front at the other. Any day when there is sun its rays catch the front of the aviary and give light and warmth. On the other hand, a shed and aviary in a wooded area tends to be extremely suitable in the Summer, but is bitterly cold in Winter. In such circumstances the author has had bantams succumb to the severe frosts which accumulate in the trees so imagine what can happen to an aviary bird.

This is not to suggest that parrot-like birds are not hardy. They will stand considerable cold and variations in weather once acclimatised, but if early breeding is required with

Yellow Fronted Kakariki (front view)
Note darker colour on breast

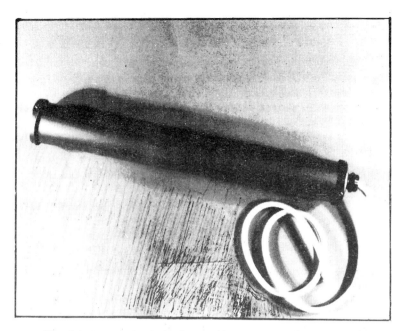

Fig. 4-4 A typical tubular heater (Courtesy: Bartholomews of Hampshire)

Fig. 4-5 A modern hospital cage (isolate mopy birds in a warm temperature)   Courtesy: Bartholomews of Hampshire.

fertile eggs from the first clutch of eggs then given them shelter from cold winds, snow and rain.

LIGHTING

Light affects birds and provides the stimulation to lay. Accordingly, the provision of adequate light is essential in two forms:

    a) Windows and netted fronts
    b) Electric light controlled by a time switch so that the desired amount of light can be given.

There is no hard and fast rule on the length of period of lighting to give. On poultry breeding and laying there has been considerable research and broadly speaking around 16–17 hours light is regarded as the standard at which to aim. This means the automatic switch is regulated to bring on the light early in the morning to cut off when natural light is adequate and then to switch back on for a further period in the evening.

An alternative is to turn on the light from a switch in the house and then turn if off last thing at night. If this is done a day of around 12 hours is the norm and many breeders have found this acceptable. Certainly if too much light is given there is a danger of stress to the birds. The intensity of light is also important; a small wattage will be adequate, say, 25 watts for an 8 x 6ft house.

Painting the building inside with a white paint will also affect the light. Lighter paints reflect light better than the darker shades so obviously it is better to use white or some other light colour. Outdoor emulsion or an oil-based paint is advisable.

PROTECTION FROM DISEASE AND PREDATORS

Birds should be protected from disease and provided common sense rules are followed there should be no problem. Some of the more obvious precautions are as follows:

    1. Feed good quality food and watch for mould or bacteria appearing.

2. Clean out food hoppers on a regular basis.

3. Remove sand or sawdust used on the floor at regular intervals. Make sure cobwebs are removed and go round breeding cages with a vacuum cleaner removing all dust — obviously removing birds before this is done. Give this a thorough clean at least once a year, preferably twice, and make sure every part is cleaned and disinfected. Also clean out cupboards and any place where vermin may lurk.

4. Spray the cages and stock with anti-mite spray and check that the birds are free from parasites. A check should be made at night with torch light to see if red mite exist.

5. Watch out for small access holes gnawed by mice or other creatures (including Parrot-like birds!) and block these. If the invasion persists place bait where mice can get it, but well away from the birds.

6. Keep adequate water in the house and change it regularly. Wash out the utensils in a mild solution of disinfectant (suitable for the purpose) and then rinse thoroughly with clean running water.

7. Have a bird bath so the birds can keep themselves clean.

8. Wash fresh green food stuff in a colander and then remove all surplus. A salad strainer is ideal for this purpose. With insecticides being used the washing is a precaution in case the green food has been sprayed. Where chick weed and other greens are grown in the garden it may be quite safe to feed without washing.

9. The outside flight should have a floor of small pebbles, or gravel, which can be washed down. Alternatively, grass may be sown, although this is not likely to last very long with a number of birds in captivity.
Concrete floors are a possibility, but these tend to be cold and should be covered with earth or sand. They at least keep out predators. On that subject it is advisable to block the bottom of a flight so that it is

predator proof. Putting wire into the ground and con-
creting under the bottom cross pieces is advisable or
rats, cats, squirrels and other nuisances will gain
access.

10. Observe the birds carefully and when illness is
apparent isolate the birds in question and where
appropriate use the hospital cage or a separate room
which is kept quite warm.

PERCHES AND RELATED EQUIPMENT

Parrots and Parrakeets are perch users and, therefore,
perches must be regarded as an essential part of the equipment of the bird-room and flight. There are a number of
places to consider:

1. Cages
   Perches are placed from front to back and arranged
   so that the occupants can jump and fly from one to
   the other.

2. Birdrooms
   Neat uniform perches may be employed, positioned
   so that some are higher than others thus enabling the
   birds to fly around.

3. Flights or outdoor aviaries
   Natural perches made from the fallen branches of pine
   trees or fruit trees provide an excellent means of giving
   all that is necessary with the added advantage of being
   pleasing in appearance. Branches containing twigs can
   be nailed into position in the corners or hanging from
   the ceiling and the birds enjoy moving from one
   section to another. Perches should be of varying sizes
   and may be oval or round. The earlier fanciers seemed
   to prefer the round type whereas today the oval-
   shaped are the first choice.

The fact remains that the size should be adequate for the
bird to exercise its feet. A typical size is 5/8ths inch
(17mm) for small birds, but parrots require at least 1 inch

(25mm) and there are some points to watch:

a) Use soft wood rather than hard and/or slippery wood.*

b) Ensure that the perch is firm so that it does not slip around when the bird alights.

c) Consider using a tapered perch which is broad at one end (say 1 inch or around 25mm) and tapers to ½inch (12mm).

d)For outside flights keep the perches away from the wire netting or cats may attack the birds whilst they are perching.

e) In siting perches in an outside flight remember to leave sufficient space for flying. Poor positioning of perches and branches may restrict the area available for flight.

SAFETY PORCHES

Access to buildings and aviaries without danger of losing birds is an essential consideration when planning accommodation. The most simple way is to have a large shed and then have a "porch" inside which allows easy access. The main compartment is kept separate with an independent door.

The disadvantage with this method is the fact that part of the bird house is wasted although this may be used to store food and equipment in regular use. Shelves can be placed on the walls and tins and boxes kept there.

Other possibilities are as follows:

1. Double Door
   A solid door outside and wire netting inside will allow access (with care) but can be hazardous when going in and out. Such an arrangement can be used to keep a bird-room cool in the summer.

---

*This is a debatable matter; if too soft some Parrakeets will quickly devour the perches, but it is their natural instinct! Fortunately Kakarikis do very little chewing.

Corner Porch

Fig. 4-6 Examples of Safety Porches. Kakarikis are very fast and can fly through an open door and escape quite easily

2. External Porches

A porch may be built on to the external door so that easy access is possible. A person entering steps inside and then closes the door before opening the main door to the bird-room without difficulty.

Many fanciers rely on an external aviary as a form of porch, but in this case great care must be taken to ensure that birds do not fly out when the door is opened.

LANDSCAPING AND AESTHETIC REQUIREMENTS

Landscaping is the designing of the aviary and the surrounding areas so that they are pleasing to the eye and more attractive to the birds. Possible additions are as follows:

1. Rustic poles for the outside flight.
2. Climbing shrubs up the side of the flight.
3. A small pond with a fountain.
4. Evergreen shrubs such as laurel and rhododendron outside the bird-room and flight.
5. Ornate structures, including brick buildings, tiled roof, elaborate windows and wrought ironwork.

The *aesthetic* requirements relate to the appearance of the aviary. Looking at a design in a negative way we can suggest that the following features should be avoided:

a) Corrugated sheets which tend to rust and look unsightly (although properly maintained they may be acceptable for the bottom of a flight).

b) Sheds which are knocked together from off-pieces of wood and appear untidy and look amateurish. If the fancier is to make his own bird-houses then they must be done to an acceptable standard.

c) Aviaries which are not maintained properly so that felt is hanging off the roof and boards are rotting for lack of paint or preservative.

PARROT-LIKE BIRDS IN AN OUTDOOR AVIARY

Parrot-like birds will do well in garden aviaries, where, contrary to generally received opinion, they will live quite comfortably all the year round, as regardless of the weather as our common sparrows, or even more so. The birds in an aviary have no anxiety about food, or any trouble in finding or getting at it; and if they have a dry place to roost in, do not seem to feel the cold at all, but will fly around and chatter as freely in the snow as if a summer sun were shining overhead.

Nesting out-of-doors

If the aviary is turfed and has shrubs growing in it, the hens will make their nests in the nest boxes provided.

Material for Nests

Parrots and parrot-like birds use bark and chips of wood for nesting. Accordingly, wood shavings would be appropriate.

Mice

Mice are the great trouble in an outdoor aviary, and they can be kept out of it only with difficulty. The little brutes seem capable of forcing their way through almost the smallest meshed wire that is made; or, if they are baffled in that direction, they will burrow underground, often making quite long tunnels, and will get into the enclosure where least expected. By placing tin all round the aviary, bent in the shape of the letter L, they are puzzled for a long time; and if all the horizontal part and half of the upright portion of the tin plate are underground, the mice will be baffled in their attempts to gain an entrance for a longer period still. I have, however, known them work their way in through a thick layer of cement, and even through a brick wall. Small mesh wire netting may also be used.

Birch-Brooms in lieu of Shrubs

If, instead of bushes for the birds to build in, birch-brooms are planted in pots, or in the soil, they can be protected by encircling the lower part of the handle with tin, up which the mice are unable to climb. but the pests can jump to a marvellous height, and think nothing of a flying leap of from 2½ft to 3ft from the wall or the wire front of the aviary into a nest.

How to get rid of Mice

Should the aviarist find that nothing will keep the vermin outside his aviary, he will have to poison them in it; but in doing this he will have to be extremely careful that his birds do not pick up any of the poison intended for their enemies. Putting in a small cage isolates the poison from the birds.

Needless to remark, when all the mice have been killed the small cage should be at once thoroughly cleansed, or better still, burned, which will effectually prevent any accident from an incautious use of it afterwards. Should more mice, after a time, appear upon the scene, they must be served in the same way, for if they are allowed about they will sadly interfere with the nesting birds, and small will indeed be the aviarist's success where the little pests exist in any number.

Cats

Cats are another intolerable nuisance to the aviariest, but can be kept out of the garden by surmounting the wall with wire-netting, 2ft 6in or 3ft high, and inclined inwards at an angle of about forty-five degrees. No cat will face that, and the birds will be left in peace.

SITE FOR AVIARY

As regards the construction of a garden aviary, it is not my intention to say much for aviaries vary infinitely, according to the taste and purse of the designer and builder; but a few general directions will not be amiss. Always select a wall (or build one, if necessary) for a background or have a strong wooden windbreaker for one wall. Lawn-aviaries open to the air all round are pretty to look at, but unsafe for birds, which are exposed in them to every blast that blows; and as the wind from some quarters is very bitter and searching, it is as well not to subject birds to its influence. The aviary should be erected against a wall that faces either south, south-west, or even south-east; but an aspect due east, or one into which north enters, must be avoided. If no other aspect is available, the fancier had better forego the delight of an outdoor aviary, and keep his birds indoors.

FOOD IN OUTDOOR AVIARY

The feeding of birds out of doors is no different to that
recommended for such of these birds as are kept in the
house; but more green stuff may be allowed, and almost
anything will do (except watercress), with the precaution
that no stale vegetable matter be left on the floor of the
aviary, which must be kept clean. If the flight part of the
aviary is turfed, the birds will want little else in the way of
green food, but some rape-seed may be advantageously
sown in a border against the wall, and covered with a wire
to keep the birds off it until it is sufficiently grown for
their use.

SHRUBS

Unless the aviary is a very large one, and not too many
birds are kept in it, there will not be much use in attempting to grow plants, or even trees, within it, for the birds will
soon pick them to pieces, not so much to eat as for sheer
mischief, or maybe occupation. The better plan is to introduce plants in pots or small tubs, which can be removed
when the plants have been disfigured, and be replaced by
others.

I have found ivy, euonymus, and the different kinds of
elder (the common, golden, silver, and parsley-leaved)
resist their attacks better than anything else. Lilac and
laburnum are both poisonous, especially the latter, and
must on no account be allowed in an aviary, no matter
what birds are kept.

SPECIAL STRUCTURE FOR
PARROT-LIKE BIRDS

Parrots and many of the smaller parrot-like birds do chew
wood and nibble the aviary until it disintegrates. This
applies to perches, nest boxes, framework of the aviary and
the house in which they live. Accordingly, although
Kakarikis are not destructive it is better to anticipate
problems and use wood of a thickness suitable for all types
of parrakeets. Alternatively, protect the inside with ply-
board or netting.

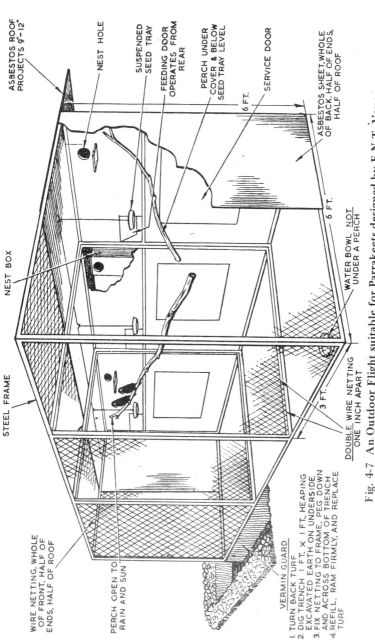

ASBESTOS ROOF PROJECTS 9"-12"

NEST HOLE

SUSPENDED SEED TRAY

FEEDING DOOR OPERATES FROM REAR

PERCH UNDER COVER & BELOW SEED TRAY LEVEL

SERVICE DOOR

ASBESTOS SHEET, WHOLE OF BACK, HALF OF ENDS, HALF OF ROOF

NEST BOX

STEEL FRAME

WIRE NETTING, WHOLE OF FRONT, HALF OF ENDS, HALF OF ROOF

PERCH OPEN TO RAIN AND SUN

WATER BOWL NOT UNDER A PERCH

DOUBLE WIRE NETTING ONE INCH APART

6 FT.

6 FT.

3 FT.

VERMIN GUARD
1. TURN BACK TURF
2. DIG TRENCH 1 FT. × 1 FT., HEAPING EXCAVATED EARTH ON UNDERSIDE
3. FIX NETTING TO FRAME, PEG DOWN AND ACROSS BOTTOM OF TRENCH
4. REFILL, RAM FIRMLY, AND REPLACE TURF

Fig. 4·7 An Outdoor Flight suitable for Parrakeets designed by E.N.T. Vane

Note: Asbestos may be replaced by one of the modern materials such as fibre   glass or perspex

An excellent aviary described by E.N.T. Vane who was a very experienced breeder of love birds is shown in Fig. 4-7. This illustrates most of the principles involved in catering for parakeets.

Obviously a steel framed aviary will allow parrots or parrakeets to be kept without fear of the outer posts being nibbled away, specialized steel framing is now available which can be bolted together and an aviary built without difficulty. "Dexion" is the main type available. In addition tubular frames may be made although these are not so easily assembled.

WOODEN STRUCTURES

Normal sheds and aviaries purchased from bird/garden centres are not usually suitable for parrot-like birds unless ordered specially or modified. Quite thick boards would be necessary — 1 inch thick (25mm) — and preferably tongue and grooved so there is nothing the birds can grasp and chew. For large parrots all wooden structures should be covered with wire netting. There is no need for this action when dealing with parrakeets.

Leaving the posts and cross pieces outside the wire is also an alternative method. Provided the birds cannot get at the wood then it cannot be destroyed.

RANGE OF FLIGHTS

Parrakeets may be housed in small aviaries, located side-by-side, thus allowing many breeding pairs to be kept. A corridor may be placed down the middle or the back of the unit thus allowing access to the sleeping quarters. Alternatively, this may be at the end of each pen.

WELFARE AND HYGIENE

An aviary with a grass surface or bare earth has some advantages, but very quickly becomes "stale" and disease-ridden.

The alternative is to have stone chips, pebbles or concrete

Fig. 4-8   An Aviary on a wall which provides shelter for Kakarikis (see text).   Ideal for a colony but for breeding, smaller flights would be used.

which becomes a permanent home for the birds.

Sometimes bird keepers suggest moving the aviary/flight around a lawn or paddock and this certainly keeps the ground fresh. It can be very inconvenient and cumbersome except for very small structures. However, it does work wonderfully when it can be applied.

A method used by the author is the regular adding of leaves, leaf mould, grass clippings, weeds and other garden bi-products to the floor of the aviary. This keeps the ground fresh, provides items of interest to the birds and is a method of disposing of leaves, etc. without difficulty. Moreover a carpet of leaves resembles the conditions birds find in the wild and therefore is quite acceptable to the birds.

SIZE OF AVIARY

For those with limited space a 6ft x 4ft flight with sheltered roost is adequate. Remember if flights are too large the Kakarikis will fly around rather wildly and lose their tameness. At breeding time the concentration should be on keeping the birds steady with minimum interference so a small flight is advisable. See Range of Flights Illustration, (Fig.4-3).

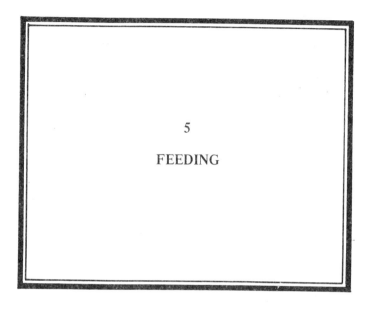

5

FEEDING

Canary seed   White Millet

Sunflower seed

Yellow Fronted Kakariki (side view)
  Blue colour is less intense and ,therefore, a yellowish
      bird is the result

Red Fronted Kakariki
  Shows the head markings very clearly

CHAPTER 5

FEEDING

VARIETY ESSENTIAL

As for all other Parrot-like birds a variety of foods should be given. An understanding of food values is essential and as a background study some relevant notes are now given.

A fancier desires to have healthy birds and this means the correct environment and adequate food which usually means a balanced diet.

The essential components are as follows:

1. Proteins

2. Carbohydrates (starches)

3. Fats

4. Water

Food technology is now also able to specify the mineral content of foods but remembering a balanced diet is essential is good enough.

In order that a balanced diet can be calculated, it is necessary that the fancier should have some knowledge of the food content of the various seeds and other foods, following which he will then be able to provide the essential

balance.   Below, is a table of seeds and other foods which
sets out the constituents:

TABLE OF APPROXIMATE FOOD VALUES

	Water	Protein	Carbo-hydrate	Fat	%
Canary Seed	15.0	14.0	52.0	5.50	86.50
Rape Seed	7.0	22.0	20.0	40.0	89
Maw Seed	9.0	19.0	18.0	45.0	91
Millet Seed	14.0	15.0	57.0	4.0	93
Linseed	9.0	23.0	23.0	24.0	79
Hemp Seed	11.0	16.0	25.0	30.0	83
Niger Seed	12.0	21.0	22.0	40.0	95
Lettuce	95.0	1.0	2.0	0.2	99.2
Dandelion	84.0	2.4	10.6	1.0	
Carrot	87.0	1.2	9.6	0.1	
Apple	83.0	0.5	15.0	Nil	98.5
Egg Yolk	47.0	15.0	Nil	33.0	95
Egg White	87.0	10.0	Nil	0.25	97.25
Sunflower Seed	6.0	24.0	21.0	49.0	100

BASIC CONSTITUENTS

There are three basic constituents necessary in the diet of all
living creatures; namely, proteins, carbohydrates and fats.
These three elements must be contained in any given diet,
and what is more important, they must be balanced against
each other if all of the dietary requirements of the birds are
to be met.

Protein
    It is frequently, and perhaps correctly, argued that
protein is the most essential constituent in the diet of any
type of bird life. Protein is the substance which builds the
muscles and which will quite literally put the meat on the
bones.

Carbohydrates
    Another essential part of the diet is the carbohydrate
content. This is the dietary element which gives energy and
which is used up rapidly by the body processes, especially
when exercise is being taken, rather in the same way as coal
is consumed in a fire.

Fats within Food

Fats are another important part of the diet. These elements supplement the carbohydrates and also generate body heat. However, excessive fat can be harmful.

From this information, it can clearly be seen that the emphasis on a balanced diet cannot be stressed too strongly. What, for example, is the point in giving a diet which is overloaded with protein, if the carbohydrates are insufficient to burn up the excess proteins? In such a case, the result would be obesity in the stock rather than a balanced type of bird. Pieces of fat are not recommended.

SPECIAL NOTES

1. **Growing feathers, beaks, toenails require an extra amount of protein and, therefore, young birds should be given a special diet containing a high level of protein.**

2. **Amino Acids** are essential for growth and, therefore, must be present in the diet. A variety of seeds is essential for the bird to achieve the level of amino acids it requires.

3. **Vitamins** These are essential to the well being of seed eaters. They are:

a) Vitamin A — fish liver oil is the best source; but greens and carrots are also essential and are taken readily. A deficiency will result in poor breeding results, constant colds (breathing difficulties), water eyes and thick mucous around the nostrils. Cod-liver oil should be mixed daily with the seed and the wild greens listed later. In addition, lettuce, spinach, kale and other fresh greens should be given. Bleached vegetables should not be given and cabbage or brussels sprouts do not give a high level of vitamin A.

b) Vitamin D — Lack of vitamin D results in leg, joint, beak and other bone growth problems (rickets). Adding cod liver oil and feeding calcium in some form will help to combat the deficiency, but sunshine is the

essential requirement. The ultra violet rays from the
sun are vital and special lamps can provide rays, but
may damage the eyes of the birds due to being too
strong. Sunshine through clean glass is not helpful
because the ultra violet rays may not pass through.

c) Vitamin E — This vitamin provides the necessary
component for reproduction. Its main source is
sprouting seeds such as wheat and certain leaf plants
such as lettuce, watercress and spinach. Egg yolk is
also a prime source. However, wheatgerm oil should
be mixed separately from cod-liver oil, although the
two can be used on seed provided they are mixed
separately.

d) Water-soluble Vitamins — Many vitamins may be
purchased in the form of a soluble solution such as
Abidec and many fanciers find that this method is
adequate. However, greenstuff and egg food are still
vital and should not be omitted.

IMPORTANCE OF FRESH SEED

If poor quality seed is fed the birds will starve or will suffer
from diseases of one sort or another. A seed is made up of
a number of parts:

a) Shell
b) Embryo (proteins and vitamins, etc.)
c) Endosperm (starches)

Each seed is a living organism which should be capable of
germinating; if not then it should not be fed to birds. The
first part to deteriorate is usually the germ part (the
embryo) which contains the proteins and without which a
bird will starve.
Problems with seeds which are deteriorating are as
follows:

a) Infested with mould and fungi.
b) Contaminated with chemicals or oil due to faulty
storage.

c) Mixed with dust and/or other undesirable elements, including mite or weevils.

d) Smelling musty or rancid.

e) Too old or kept in warm humid conditions. A cool well ventilated atmosphere is desirable.

SPROUTING SEEDS

Many bird fanciers believe wholeheartedly that sprouted seed should be an integral part of the diet of cage birds. It is agreed that sprouting reduces the starch and increases the protein and in addition makes the seed more easily digested. They spend hours each month preparing and feeding the sprouted seeds and certainly many birds seem to relish the wet food.

In recent times doubt has been cast on the wisdom of using sprouted seed and whilst there is not conclusive proof that the practice is harmful the following facts should be considered:

1. Soaking brings about a chemical reaction in the seed and changes the starch to sugar. This in itself is not harmful but if the seeds are left in the water, without adequate exposure to the air, they begin to deteriorate. In fact, if left longer than 24 hours the seed will begin to die. An experiment carried out in the USA found that birds fed with seeds soaked for 48 hours would not lay.

2. Many of the proteins may be released into the water.

3. From observations made it would appear that soaked seeds do not digest properly. Soaking appears to give them some kind of protection against the digestive juices; in fact, nestlings fed by their parents will usually pass the soaked seeds through their system without any change in composition.

SPECIAL NOTE:

Most of the arguments against seeds germinated are levelled against *soaked* seeds. Accordingly, if sprouted seeds are to be fed then they should be germinated on a stainless steel or plastic dish and kept *damp* (not soaked) by means of gauze which rests in water. Absolute cleanliness is essential to avoid contamination.

CONDITIONS REQUIRING DIFFERENT OR SUPPLEMENTED FOOD

When feeding birds it is essential to consider the following:

1. Normal feeding for healthy stock.
2. Feeding for breeding.
3. Food for moulting.
4. Supplements or special food for periods of stress, e.g. when moulting or when sick.

NORMAL FEEDING

The comments made earlier apply to this situation. A *balanced* diet is essential and feed regularly so that the birds have ample food without standing around too long.

When dealing with domesticated birds such as poultry we can state precisely what quantity is necessary for growing, laying and so on. Around 4oz. per laying hen will be fed. This is a precise measure. However, with cage birds the amount eaten is not proportionate to the relative weight of fowl and, say, canaries or parrots. Some food they will peck out of the hoppers, others they will leave and there is no standardisation as for poultry. A parrot prefers different food from a budgerigar although they belong to the same family. Each bird fancier must find out the likes and dislikes of his birds and feed accordingly.

FOOD FOR MOULTING

A great deal is written about the problems of the moult and yet in the correct environment there is generally no problem. The fact remains that the growing of feathers requires

Fig. 5-1 Food Hopper which holds around 6lb of Seed
(Courtesy: Haines Aviary Economy)

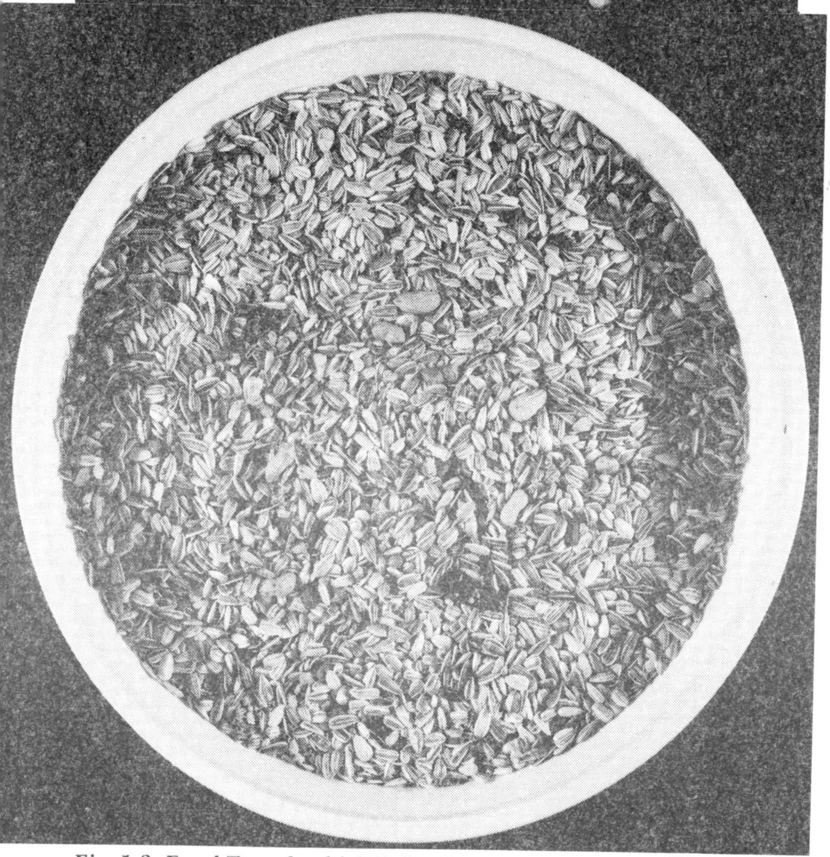

Fig. 5-2 Food Trough which Kakarikis may prefer for scratching in
the seed.

extra protein and vitamins. Soft food is usually recommended and tonic seeds should also be given.

The annual shedding of feathers takes place as the weather changes and becomes colder. In the UK this occurs around the middle of September and goes on for a few weeks; it may occur earlier or later, but usually an attempt is made to have birds back in condition for the November shows.

Some fanciers have special cages for moulting birds, whereas others simply separate the cocks. When birds are transferred they should be taken in pairs or threes so they are placed in their new abode together thus avoiding conflict when single birds are placed in a cage at different times.

At the *early stages* of the moulting period feed a plain diet and water until feathers begin to fall. A bird is through the moult when the new head feathers are fully grown.

Soft food should be given twice weekly. During the moult there should be adequate ventilation and moderate exercise. A plentiful supply of the greenstuff is essential.

Additional Notes

For the novice additional notes are now added compiled by a well known bird keeper:

1. Green Food

   Some breeders advocate a liberal supply of green food for breeding birds, while others look upon it as little short of a deadly poison; and here it may be remarked that both sides are right to a certain extent, for much depends upon the kind and quality of the green stuff supplied to the birds.

   Nature provides a valuable part of the supplementary food required by Parrakeets. Greenstuff is a vital part of the diet and wild seeds help to provide oil and other essentials for beautiful plumage.

   The main green foods are as follows:

   (a) Chickweed which is very popular and nutritious (although some fanciers do not like to feed chickweed)

   (b) Dandelion which provides many essentials such as calcium, iron and magnesium

   (c) Mustard seed

   (d) Plantain

(e) Shepherd's purse
(f) Teazle
(g) Dock

A little should be given once a day and should be varied to stimulate the appetite.
Important: wild seeds are those taken from dock, maw, presacaria, gold of pleasure and plantain

2. Basic Foods
Food stuffs of seeds of various types supplemented with vitamins, oils and minerals. In addition, wild plants and fruit should be given on a regular basis, thus keeping the birds in peak condition.
A balanced diet is essential and this should be formulated on the basis of whether dealing with birds for breeding or when moulting, or for normal feeding.

Birds will acquit themselves of their parental duties to the satisfaction of their owner. But sometimes they will not, and it is only fair to say that there are birds that no plan or system of feeding will induce to attend to their offspring for more than a few days, or a week or two at the outside.

PREPARING EGG-FOOD

To return to the preparation of egg-food. Take the newly-laid egg of a domestic fowl, and boil it for ten minutes; then take it out of the saucepan and let it stand till cold. Then remove the shell, take the whole of the yolk and half the white with an equal weight of biscuit, put the ingredients in a basin, well mix until they are thoroughly incorporated and form a crumbly paste.
Except in very hot weather, the egg and biscuit may be blended together at one time, and will suffice for a pair of breeding birds and their young for a day; but if the weather is close and sultry it will be better to prepare this food twice daily, and to remove any that is left over from what may be called the first helping when the second is placed in the cage.

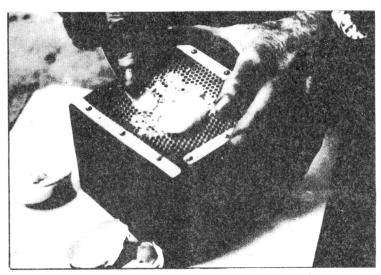

Fig. 5-3 Preparing Egg Food for Mixing (see text)

Fig. 5-4 Sprouting Seeds for Feeding

FEEDING WITHOUT EGG

We may now glance at the "no-egg system" of feeding, premising that it will not always answer in the case of birds that have been accustomed to a more stimulating kind of diet. If it is desired to cut down on the protein, it is advisable to mix crushed biscuit with a little milk; but water will do as well to mix the ground biscuit into a paste of suitable consistency. Old bread (a few days old) may be soaked in milk or water and squeezed out and fed a little at a time.

SOAKED SEED

So far so good; now we come to the most important part of the system. The seed — the best quality obtainable — is to be put to soak in cold fresh water. When taken from the vessel in which it has been soaked, the seed should be wiped dry in a towel or other cloth or it should be strained thoroughly as part of the process. If this precaution is neglected the seed will stick together in a lump, will be difficult for the birds to get at, and will, moreover, be liable to turn sour. The seed must be prepared from day to day and if put to soak in the morning, when the birds are being attended to, will be ready by the same hour on the following day. Regularity in this respect reduces the "trouble" to a minimum.

SEED-HOPPERS

Several kinds of seed-hoppers have been invented, with the object of guarding against waste. Many birds make a practice of scattering their seed — in search, no doubt, of something of which they are in want — and these hoppers are useful in their way, especially that shown in Figure 5-1, but as much care is necessary to keep the contents clean and free from dust in their case as in that of the ordinary kind.

SIFTING SEED

All seed should be sifted and winnowed before it is offered to the birds. A convenient way is to take a small box, remove the bottom, and replace it by a piece of perforated metal. The box should then be half-filled with the seed, the lid shut down, and the whole agitated with a rotary movement until no more dust falls from the box, when the contents will be found to be free from particles of extraneous and often hurtful matter. Some chaff, however, may yet remain, and this can be readily got rid of by slowly pouring the contents of the box into some other receptacle the box being held as far above the other vessel as may be convenient. If this is done in the open air the light particles of chaff, etc. will be blown away by the wind; but if the operation is performed in the house, it can be assisted by blowing on it.

WINNOWING MACHINE

For those who would like to make sure that the seed is treated thoroughly a special Winnowing Machine is available (see Figure 5-5).

STRICT CLEANLINESS ESSENTIAL

Needless to say, all vessels containing food or water must be kept as scrupulously clean as if they were intended for the owner's own use, and for that reason anything in the way of a receptacle with corners should be avoided, and nothing be used but a rounded cup. A little exercise of ingenuity will enable the amateur to fix the cup securely in the cage so that it will be in no danger of being overturned by the birds. Special lids can also be fitted over the water jars.

IONISERS

For fanciers who wish to remove dust, bacteria and other harmful spores from the air an Ioniser is available. This is illustrated in Figure 5-6 and can be recommended to those fanciers who keep a number of birds, especially when the birds are kept indoors.

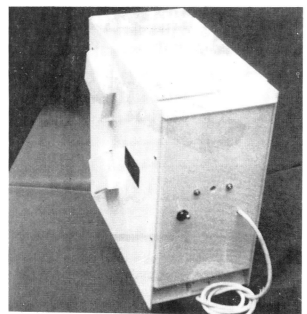

Fig. 5-5 Winnowing Machine (Haines Aviary Economy)

Fig. 5-6 Ioniser (Courtesy: Prestige Tehnology Ltd) for Indoor Bird
Rooms

WATER

An important point, and one that is too often overlooked, is to keep the drinking water pure and clean, for birds, especially when egg-fed, are apt to quickly spoil it by dipping their beaks into the fountain or cup while particles of food are still adhering to their mandibles. It will be as well, particularly in hot weather, to change the water and cleanse the vessel that holds it several times a day, for the particles of egg and other food quickly decompose, and are apt to give rise to troublesome diarrhoea in both old and young.

GRIT

Calcium is essential for the development of egg shells and as part of the diet. In addition insoluble grit must be provided for digesting the food; e.g. flint at the appropriate size.

The mixture to be given should include:

1. Cuttle-fish bone
2. Washed river sand
3. Oyster shell
4. Charcoal finely ground

GETTING THE CORRECT BALANCE

As noted above the typical foods contain different proportions of protein, carboyhdrate and fat. Getting the correct balance is important but also difficult.

Like humans, birds have periods when they like one form of food rather than another. The weather, time of year, whether breeding or moulting all make a difference.

In addition there is **habit** — what foods have been fed in the past, especially in the early stages of development. When new birds are acquired there is always difficulty in getting the mixture correct and, indeed, it is advisable to ask the previous owner for details of the diet.

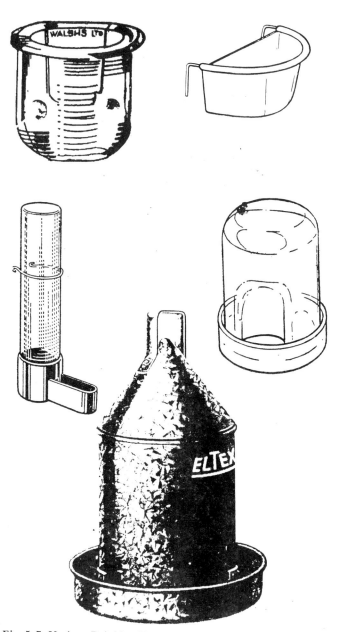

Fig. 5-7 Various Drinking Vessels. A small galvanised water fountain
is quite suitable for weekly changing of water;
a hanging cup may be used if filled each day.

Mixed Seeds for Parrakeets

**Fasten with
Bull Dog Clip
to Upright in
Aviary**

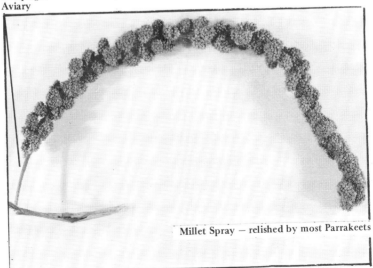

Millet Spray — relished by most Parrakeets

Fig. 5-8 Typical Seeds for Parrakeets — some breeders do not like too much Sunflower Seed, but the author has found they relish a good supply

As a rough guide it is usual to divide mixtures as follows:

1. Large Parrots
(eg, Macaws, Amazons, Cockatoos, African Greys, etc)

Give a mixture consisting of large nutritious foods such as sunflower seeds, nuts, maize, hemp, canary seed, millet, wheat and niger.

Opinions differ on the proportions. Sunflower seeds should form a substantial part. One well known breeder suggests 65% whereas another believes that 40% is about right with the balance being made up of canary seed and other food. For example:

Grey Parrot

	%
Canary	30
Millet	5
Hemp	5
Sunflower	50
Oats	5
Peanuts	5
	100%

Note: Lories eat nectar and fruit so must be treated differently. Fruit should be given to all species on a regular basis.

2. Parrakeets and Smaller Parrots
(eg, Parrakeets, Love Birds, Kakarikis, Cockatiels)

A similar mixture to the above but with more of the smaller seeds. The smaller birds should **not** be given too much sunflower seed or hemp.

Example: Kakarikis

	%
Canary	50
Millet	20
Peanuts	10
Sunflower	10
Safflower	10
	100%

In addition various fruits, greens and softfood would be given as described earlier. Softfoods, including egg as described, would also be essential. A favourite is poultry corn. The author throws a handful in the pen each morning and the Kakarikis love it.

BASIC RULES – SUMMARY

1. Feed on a regular basis and clear husks away every few days. Some bird keepers maintain a small collection of other birds such as doves, quail, bantams which clear away discarded food. Obviously a large enough aviary will be essential.

2. Provide an adequate and varied diet:
   (a) Mixed seeds and nuts as above
   (b) Fruit; eg Pears, grapes and apples, bananas, blackberries and dates
   (c) Softfood such as stale bread – not mouldy, soaked and then the liquid pressed out to make it crumbly (not doughy) or egg food (described earlier)
   (d) Green foods such as (i) lettuce, spinach and garden peas   (ii) wild plants and seeds there from including chick-weed, dock, persicaria and plantain
   (e) Root vegetables; eg, carrots
   (f) Soaked seeds and also sprouting seeds

   Do not leave food around too long and feed fresh fruit which is not too ripe. Bananas which have gone to pulp are frequently seen in aviaries and are unattractive to most birds.

3. Provide other essentials such as:

   (a) Grit, cuttlefish bone, etc.
   (b) Water
   (c) Vitamins

4. Use suitable food and water utensils so food is not wasted

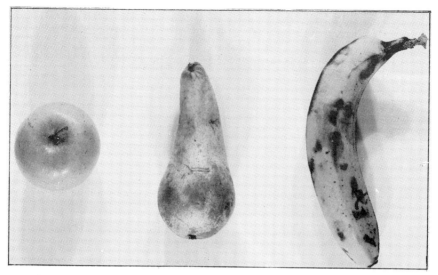

Apple   Pear   Banana

Fruit — remove before stale or too ripe (daily clearance advisable)
Parrakeets are fruit eaters so this part of the diet is vital

**Cut up apples into quarters (unlike Ring Necks Kakarikis will not
tackle whole apples).**

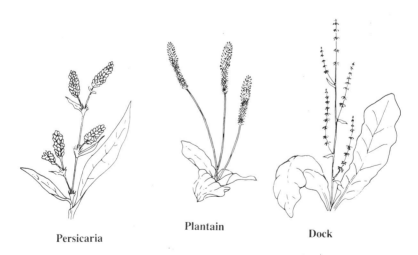

Persicaria   Plantain   Dock

Wild plants which are best changed each day

Fig. 5-9 Daily Additions to the Diet

5. Provide a bath so that birds can splash around and   bathe themselves. A small pond in the aviary can be useful and decorative. Kakarikis love to splash in water. A plastic bowl with a brick in the middle is ideal — a small pond with an island!

All food should be clean and wholesome. Fruit such as apples should be placed on spikes; eg, nails, so they cannot roll around the aviary.

Greenstuff should be rinsed to remove possible eggs of worms or other parasites and also to eliminate any chemicals where the plants may have been sprayed. Badly frosted greens should not be fed.

6

UNDERSTANDING
BIRD ANATOMY

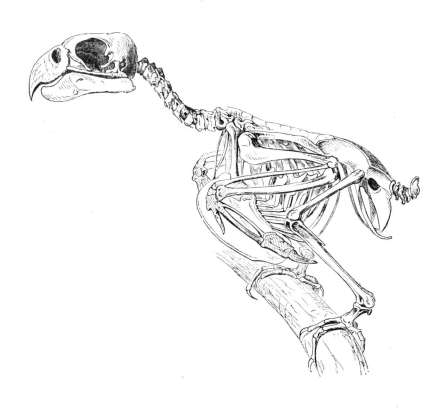

Fig. 6-1 The Skeleton of A Parrot-like Bird
Note: Obviously different species show varying features; eg, larger
heads. Kakarikis have fairly small skulls and beaks

CHAPTER 6

UNDERSTANDING BIRD ANATOMY

A bird's anatomy may be viewed from two aspects:

1. The **internal organs** responsible for providing sustenance and the means of developing eggs in the female bird.

    2. The **outward** form upon which any *standard* is based.

An understanding of both is vital. The provision of appropriate food, water and minerals is vital to success. Unsuitable foods do not provide the essentials and lead to health problems. For the chicks higher protein food develops bone, flesh and feathers and ensures rapid growth.

The outward shape, including the face, beak, crest, neck, body, legs, wings and feathers show the breed of bird. The external shape and appearance indicate important facts on the type of bird.

THE SKELETON AND INTERNAL ORGANS

The internal organs of a bird fit within a structure of bones the skeleton (Figure 6-1). Knowledge of the principal parts are:

1. **Breastbone**
    The breastbone or *sternum* is a vital part of the body. It protects the internal organs as well as a foundation for the flesh and muscles which operate the wings.

2. **Wings**
    The wings provide the means of flying. Their position-ing is of vital importance in determining *style* and *posture*; when carried high the thighs are revealed and

DIGESTIVE SYSTEM

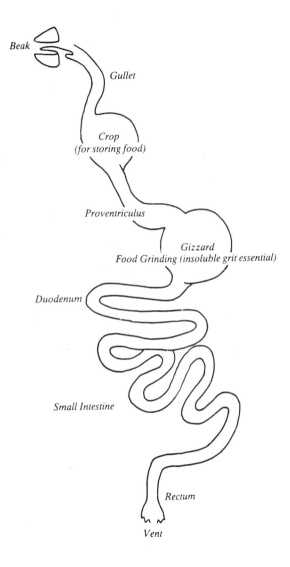

Fig. 6-2 The Digestive System

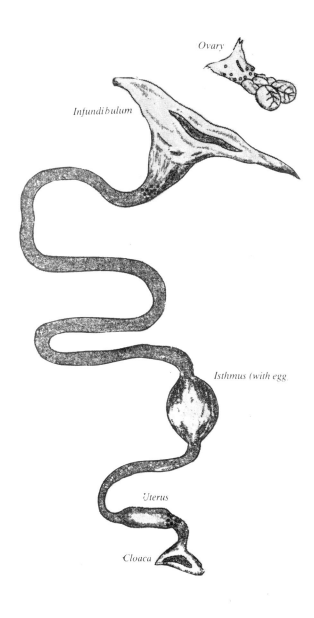

Fig. 6-3 Female Bird Reproductive System

the result is a taller looking bird.

3. Legs and Feet
The legs and feet provide the means of walking, perching and climbing. They should be free from bumps or
enlarged scales.

4. Head
The head is mounted upon the neck which is quite
flexible. At the front of the skull is the beak made up
of the upper and lower mandible. Size and shape of
head is of vital importance. Parrots and parrot-like
birds have very strong, curved beaks which they use
for chewing wood and crushing seeds and nuts.

ANATOMY

The functioning of the bird is relatively simple and yet is
an incredible process. Food is converted into flesh and/or
eggs which, after incubation become chicks which rapidly
grow into adult birds, and then at about 6–9 months of
age they too become producers, thus repeating the process.
The main parts are as follows:

1. Beak
Food is picked up by a bird and "shelled" as
appropriate before proceeding down the throat into
the crop, a bag made of skin, and from there it goes
on to the gizzard.

2. Crop and Gizzard
The cop is the store for food just taken and this passes
into a passageway known as a proventriculis (or ventri-
culus) before passing into the gizzard. The latter is an
almost solid organ which masticates food so that it can
be digested.

3. Intestines
From the gizzard food passes into the intestines and
after due processing is passed out through the rectum
(or vent).

Within the digestive framework there are:

(a) **Liver** in which is found the gall bladder which stores the bile;

(b)**Kidneys** (two which filter the liquids and excrete uric acid.

Blood and Air Circulation

The blood is circulated by the contraction and expansion of the heart which is usually likened to a pump which has four chambers — the upper two named "auricles" and the lower two the "ventricles".

The bird breathes through its nostrils or mouth into the bronchial tubes and lungs. The arterial veins from the heart pass through the lungs thus allowing the circulating blood to be oxygenated.

REPRODUCTIVE SYSTEM

For successful reproduction both male and female should be in good health and well fed. Eggs should become fertile within a few days of male and female being placed together, but generally a period of ten days is considered to be a safe waiting time.

The female has two ovaries only one of which usually develops. In addition, there is the oviduct, a long twisting tube consisting of two parts through which a yolk passes, adding the various parts ("white", membranes and shell) until the egg falls into the cloaca or egg pouch.

Opinions on how long the process takes vary, but generally around eighteen hours is regarded as the cycle time. Within the ovary there are many embryo eggs (oocytes) — more than 1500 have been counted in a fowl's ovary. These develop so that a few large yolks ripen (usually about five) until one is ready to go into the oviduct for development into the egg.

The male bird "treads" the hen and thereby fertilises the eggs. He discharges semen from testes into two ducts and thence into the oviduct of the female when the mating takes place.

THE EGG SHELL – GENERAL NOTES

The outer shell of the egg is made up of three distinct layers:

1. Cuticle
   A fine coating which gives the egg its lustre or bloom.

2. Palisade or spongy Layer
   The bulk of the shell (approx. 2/3rds of the thickness).

3. Mammillary
   The INNER part.

The shell is very strong and relative to its size can withstand great pressure (Hen egg 60 gramme 4.1 kilos breaking strength, whereas a small fresh egg, 1 gramme in weight will withstand 0.1 kilo).

Creating the Shell

The top-quality shell comes from the healthy bird, managed in a suitable environment with the appropriate type of food, water and other essentials.

Birds flying out of doors with access to grass, vegetation, earth and other natural objects usually produce eggs of good quality. The calcium carbonate required to produce the shell comes from the food eaten and from sand, stones, leaves and other small items picked up. Limestone is the main ingredient for the shell substance and yet nowhere will it be obviously available.

Proper functioning requires the quantity absorbed to be considered and must be consumed by each hen according to her requirements. Birds kept in cages or aviaries, may be given fine oyster shell and limestone provided in suitable hoppers. If topped up regularly the hens will regulate their own consumption.

Birds in the wild eat grit each day. Ornithologists have found that game birds consume considerable quantities of grit even though they may lay only around 30 eggs per season. Obviously, though, egg production is not the only consideration. Adequate nutrition requires an efficient digestive system and this depends upon the functioning of

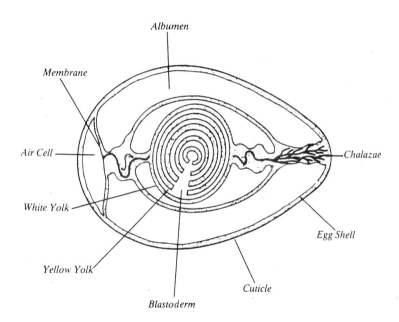

Albumen

Membrane

Air Cell

White Yolk

Yellow Yolk

Blastoderm

Chalazae

Egg Shell

Cuticle

Fig. 6-4 The Egg — Greatly Enlarged

Note: Terms are self-explanatory except the CHALAZAE which is a
special part of the albumen.

the gizzard. This will function without insoluble grit, but is much more effective when birds are able to eat as much grit as required.

Pheasants, doves, partridges, geese and other birds have been observed taking their daily intake of gravel or other grit. Percentages found in the crops of pheasant was 26 per cent and in Hungarian partridge it was 40 per cent. These were much higher than for grouse (6 per cent) and Mallard (13 per cent). They were not regarded as conclusive evidence of the normal intake percentages, but rather they confirm the need for regular supplies of grit.

SIZE OF GRIT

When grit is fed to birds it should be appropriate to the size of bird. Birds such as grouse or pheasant should be supplied with small granules which they can consume easily in their gizzards should the supply be cut off. Smaller birds should be given grit which is rather like coarse sand.

Parrakeets should be given small size grit of the flinty type as well as limestone grit.

THE MEMBRANE

Within the shell there are two membranes:

1. Inner Membrane
   Which surrounds the albumen.

2. Outer Membrane
   Which adheres to the inside of the outer membrane except at the broad end occupied by the air space.

Air Space

The air space is non-existent in a new laid egg, but gradually appears, taking as little as two minutes (or longer) depending upon the rate at which the egg cools. It supplies a vital air supply to the chicks and without it they would die.

7

PRODUCING
THE EGGS
AND
BREEDING

Fig. 7-1 A Typical Nest of Eggs and a Kakariki Egg (actual size)

CHAPTER 7

PRODUCING THE EGGS
AND BREEDING

REPRODUCTION

In common with all other reproducing is the laying of eggs, which have been previously fertilised, followed by incubation.

A number of stages are involved and in the wild state the birds adapt themselves to the environment in which they live. In domestication the birds are affected by the conditions created by the breeder who can stimulate production by means of artificial light, special foods and top class accommodation.

An understanding of the various stages involved is essential for the sound management of parrots and parrot-like birds. Fortunately the functioning of the egg forming and laying mechanism is very much the same . . . whether domestic fowl, pheasants, parrots, budgerigars or canaries. There are differences, but these are not fundamental to the general pattern followed.

Differences which may be found are:

1. **Laying a set of eggs known as a "clutch"**
2. **Size of eggs**
3. **Incubation period**

THE CLUTCH

Those birds not highly domesticated tend to lay one, two or more clutches in a year, whereas the domesticated duck or fowl may lay practically every day (except when moulting).

The size of clutch and frequency of laying also varies.

For example, the domesticated pigeon lays two eggs but may produce say, eight pairs of chicks in a season. Generally the breeder sticks to one or two broods in a season although if the bird-room is heated as many as three nests may be laid and hatched.

Some birds lay a single egg in the clutch (e.g.; auk), whereas others lay two (pigeons) and some produce as many as twenty eggs (e.g. pheasant). Small birds such as parrots lay between 2 and 9 eggs, the norm being around five. Later clutches in a season may have a smaller number of eggs.

SIZE OF EGGS

The size of eggs vary according to the body weight of the bird, but not in direct proportion. For example, in the domestic fowl Indian Game which are quite stout, heavy birds lay relatively small eggs compared with the Mediterranean breeds such as White Leghorn.

The parrot egg comes out at various sizes and weights which is not surprising considering the variety of species in existence.

Because of the delicate structure of the egg and the bird which creates it, a special watchfulness must be observed at breeding time. Egg binding is a common complaint amongst some species and a mopey, out-of-sorts hen may be suffering from the problem. She tries to pass the egg but, suffering from a form of lethargy, she struggles and struggles until she becomes quite ill. Olive oil or vaseline may lubricate the vent and remove the problem but any further, more drastic treatment, may result in breaking the egg or causing severe inflammation. Sound diet and healthy birds generally avoid this condition so there is a need to understand food requirements.

INCUBATION PERIODS

Incubation periods vary a great deal with the smaller birds taking a shorter period. For example, some larger parrots take 28 days whereas the Kakariki averages 21 days, compared with a bantam 19, ducks 28, pigeons 16–18 days, geese 28–35 days and the ostrich around 41 days. Indeed amongst water-fowl and pheasants the period varies from one species to another.

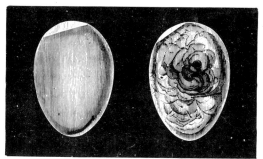

BARREN EGG.   FERTILE EGG.

Fig. 7-2 Barren and Fertile Egg Compared
Once incubation starts the embryo will grow. Great care must be taken with Kakariki eggs because they are very fragile, but if a test is considered essential at 10 days look for the blood vessels and the definite air space. Be very careful before discarding eggs.

LAYING

Once the breeding season arrives the Kakariki will lay her first egg and then follow on laying an egg every other morning until the clutch of around five eggs is laid.

If care is not taken Kakarikis may try to breed too frequently which should be avoided.

BREEDiNG

Time for Breeding

The period for breeding varies according to the climate and, therefore the rules for the U.K. cannot be followed for, say, Australia, certain parts of the U.S.A. and the warmer climates of some European countries. Generally speaking for temperature climates the mating season extends from the **middle of February** to **July**, with April the most popular month.

Early youngsters are preferred because they always seem to thrive well, making the most of the better weather when they are feathered and learning to fly. Obviously, though, the birds must be well sheltered and provided with heat or they will not respond. In fact, if they do lay in cold weather with no artificial heat it may be found that the eggs are infertile.

Planning the Operation

Even after admitting the need for early eggs there are many fanciers who believe that too early a start can have unfortunate consequences. **Natural Breeding** as opposed to **induced breeding** is urged by these fanciers. It is argued that forcing the birds to lay too early results in more "clear" eggs which is a waste of time and effort.

The fact is that both the Natural and Induced methods can claim successes so we have to look at the reasons why breeders manage to get good results. In essence there is need to prepare well in advance and not rush the birds.

Stages are as follows:

1. In January start to feed the birds supplementary good quality foods in terms of protein. This consists of egg food which is fed once a week initially and then four times in March.

2. Continue to feed the normal seed, but also give sprouting seeds.

3. Feed chick weed, water-cress and other plant food as it comes available, see Chapter 6.

From experience it will be known what the birds will eat readily and this should be fed until both cock and hen are in condition.

Pairing-Up

The birds to be used for breeding should be paired up when they appear ready:

Cock:

The male Kakariki will tend to be of heavier build with a fairly full head. He will display a certain amount of vigour, even aggression.

When the vent is examined it will be seen to be more prominent than the hen. A cock in his second season is probably the best choice, but some breeders have considerable success with young birds with no previous experience.

Hen: A hen in good condition, ready for pairing, should be in good feather and the vent should be flat with a protruding abdomen, the latter being full and round. The inspection is done by blowing up the feathers in the area to be examined.

Various signs will indicate that they are about to breed. They will be friendly to each other, the cock being attentive and fussing around his mate. He will also feed the hen by regurgitation and flutter around her, to attract attention.

The hen will also show signs of wanting to breed by crouching down. She will also squat on the perch with her wings fluttering. Such are the ways of Nature!

Young birds will be mature enough at around 9 months old.

INTRODUCING THE NEST BOXES*

When there is harmony in the aviary it is time to introduce the nest boxes. These are made in various types and, therefore, consideration should be given to the best one to use; for example:

a) Hollowed log
b) Plywood box or similar; eg, Plastic
c) Metal container

Use one which is reasonably deep and not too hot in warm weather. Take great care in providing suitable nest boxes.

The nest box should be fitted firmly to the side of the birdroom in a corner or other quiet spot, or hang from a hook or similar device.

Nest Box Lining
A nest turf may be placed in the box as a base for the nest

* Controversy surrounds nest boxes. Some fanciers specify all kinds of variations, size, positioning, etc. Try to give an adequate size in a quiet position and there should be no problem.

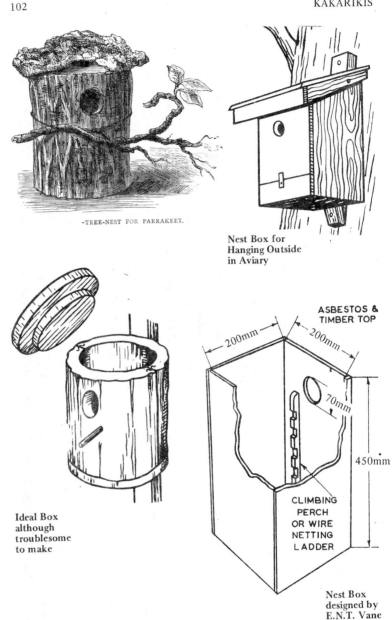

-TREE-NEST FOR PARRAKEET.

Nest Box for
Hanging Outside
in Aviary

Ideal Box
although
troublesome
to make

ASBESTOS &
TIMBER TOP

200mm   200mm

70mm

450mm

CLIMBING
PERCH
OR WIRE
NETTING
LADDER

Nest Box
designed by
E.N.T. Vane

Fig. 7-3 Nest Boxes (Upright type is preferred)
Parrakeets prefer to nest in boxes which simulate hollowed out trees.
Entrance hole should be approximately 70mm in diameter.

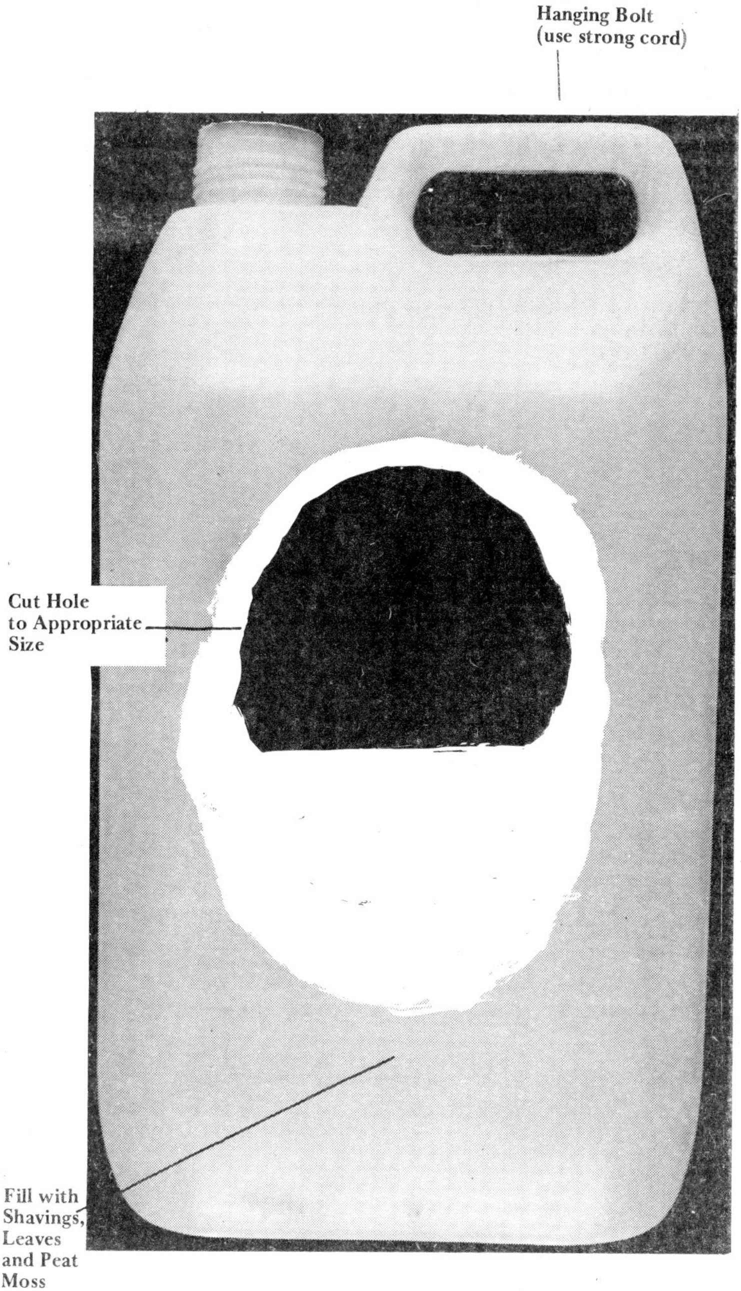

Hanging Bolt
(use strong cord)

Cut Hole
to Appropriate
Size

Fill with
Shavings,
Leaves
and Peat
Moss

Fig. 7-4 Plastic Nest Box made from a discarded container: approx.
measurements 10ins x 10ins x 16ins deep

proper. This turf may be dug from the garden. Some fanciers simply supply peat moss and shavings.

As noted earlier the hen will lay between three and eight eggs.

The materials which may be provided are:

1. Peat moss or leaves
2. Bark
3. Shavings/sawdust
4. Soil

As a precaution against mite it is usual to dust underneath the turf with insect powder thus anticipating a likely invasion once the hen is sitting hard.

A fresh turf will provide the necessary dampness in a nest box.

EGG BINDING

A common problem is for a hen to have difficulty in laying eggs which is passing down the oviduct. She will be seen to be out of sorts with ruffled feathers and looking miserable. Egg binding may be caused by one or more of a number of factors:

1. Soft-shelled eggs due to inadequate or unsuitable calcium grit
2. Hen too fat and out of condition
3. Incorrect diet
4. Overheating in the bird-room and nest box
5. Constipation causing a partial blockage of the oviduct by exerting pressure
6. Old hen who is not strong enough to lay the egg
7. Egg too large to be expelled

Parrakeets can be very difficult with egg binding so prompt attention is essential.

Possible Solutions
Once egg binding has occurred there are many possibilities:

a) Do nothing initially, but place the hen into a hospital cage at a temperature of around 75 to 80°F (25°C) and provided not too serious the egg will be laid by the next morning.

b) Oil the vent by using a fine brush (castor or olive oil). This may be followed by steaming the vent over hot water (not too hot) placed in a jar or jug with muslin over the top. After five minutes the egg should appear.

c) Apply the "expression method" of expelling the egg. This method was advocated by Victorian bird fanciers **and is not to be recommended** to the amateur fancier who will probably break the egg. GREAT CAUTION MUST BE EXERCISED.*

EXPRESSION METHOD

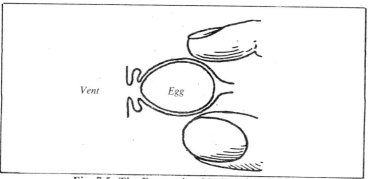

Fig. 7-5 The Expression Method (see text)

Briefly, the method, which is illustrated above, was: bird on its back in left hand, head towards right hand; finger and thumb placed on sides of egg near vent and drawn backwards with gentle pressure on the egg to be sure of pushing aside the intestines and oviduct which lie partially over its surface. When sufficiently drawn back the finger and thumb holding egg between are gently, slowly and firmly pushed forwards towards the vent and the ease with which the egg is expressed into the palm of the hand is magical. I do not think it causes more pain than usual; it is certainly qucker and therefore must relieve the bird of hours of suffering, and as far as I know it is free from any ill effects as it simply imitates nature and supplies the defective expulsive efforts.

Great care and gentleness are required, and a delicate touch is a very great asset in the accomplishment of the manoeuvre. On no account should the egg be pinched between the finger and thumb, or it will be broken and is then more difficult to get away. Personally, I have done it, i.e., broken it, and got it away successfully, and on the rare occasions that I had an accident, once only,

*This method has been used very successfully with canaries, but we have had no call to use it for Kakarikis.

as far as I can remember, it was due to my not taking sufficient time and care in the correct placing of the finger and thumb. Only sufficient pressure should be made to prevent the egg going backwards between the finger and thumb, and the whole arrangement of the egg and finger and thumb should be pushed forwards towards the vent. If the first attempt fails to extrude the egg, it will have at least partially dilated the oviduct end, and a series of gentle pressures forward with re-adjustments of thumb and finger will push the egg down until its greatest diameter has passed the resistance in front, and the manipulation will succeed. The fancier who has a very heavy hand and not a delicate sense of touch would be wise to ask a fellow fancier who is better in these respects to attempt it for him. I think it would be justifiable, if the usually suggested means failed, for him to attempt it if he is careful and the condition of the hen is such that death must ensue if left unrelieved.

EGG EATING

Sometimes by accident a bird will crack an egg, taste the contents with her beak, and then become an egg eater. Such birds are a curse because they destroy all the work and effort put into a breeding season.

Possible preventive measures are as follows:

1. Remove the eggs quickly when laid and replace with dummy eggs.

2. Fill an egg with strong mustard and put sellotape over the holes. Once she has tasted the unsavoury mixture she should stop the habit.

3. Make sure that the birds have adequate water, minerals greenstuff and seed.

4. Use specially designed nest box with allows an egg to drop through to a safe box.

EGG-EATING COCKS

The only time when interference with the eggs is necessary is in the rare instances when the cock evinces a disposition to meddle with them. Then, indeed, it will be safer to take each away as soon as it is laid, and to introduce one of plastic in its place, doing so each morning, until the hen has laid her last egg, and settled herself down to her duty. The artificial egg should then be taken away, and her own eggs restored to her to incubate in peace, in the absence of the cock, placed elsewhere.

ABNORMAL EGGS

If a hen lays large eggs or abnormally shaped eggs she should be placed on a diet of plain seed, bread and milk and dandelion to act as a tonic. After 2 weeks she should be down to an acceptable size and thinned of excess fat, which will allow her to resume normal laying.

THE HATCH

Kakariki chicks are slow to mature. They are tiny at birth and covered in down of a greyish colour. Around 14 days or a little earlier they can see and begin to utter sounds. Feathering proceeds slowly until around 30 days they are fairly well covered.

Avoid all interference with the hen around the nineteenth day and the following, for the all-important event of hatching should now be taking place. This is the testing time for all previous efforts and the success (or otherwise) of the bird management will soon be apparent.

If success is to attend the hatch the fancier will be greeted with a faint cheep from the newly hatched chicks. Do not remove or frighten the hen from the nest but feed her and hope she will leave her family for food. In such cases the nest can be examined and if the eggs are pipping just leave them and wait for the hatching to continue.

When the hatch is delayed a dilemma exists. Should the eggs be tested for infertility or should the chicks be assisted to hatch. Opinions differ on this question and probably the safest way is to wait 3–4 days before doing anything. Nature should be allowed to take its course for generally only strong chicks emerge from this process. Those taken from the eggs usually die. Remember Parrakeet eggs will hatch at different dates over a period.

BATHS

Many fanciers do not allow a bath while a bird is sitting, but this I think is a mistake, and accounts at least for some cases of failure in hatching in hot weather. A bath should always be available for use. A shallow pan makes the best bath for the bird-room.

WEANING

Weaning is the term used for the process of taking the young birds away from their parents and teaching them to fend for themselves. This process is begun when the chicks are about 6–7 weeks old.

The hen feeds the chicks and she in turn may be fed by the cock who occasionally may also feed the chicks as they mature.

It is true that the earlier the chicks are removed then the earlier they will become self-sufficient, but if there is any doubt then it is wiser to leave them with their parents for a little longer.

WEANING FOOD

When the chicks have left the nest for the first time at about 4 weeks, bread and milk should be supplied at mid-day. The probability is that the chicks will make the attempt to feed themselves and will become familiar with this type of food. The chances of their becoming self-sufficient very quickly when they are removed from their breeding pens are thereby greatly increased.

At the point at which the chicks are removed from the breeding pens, bread and milk should be offered in a wet, crumbly state to begin with, along with egg food. The bread and milk should be changed at least twice each day to prevent the chicks from taking sour food, as also should the soft food. After a few days it will be noticed that the chicks will begin to eat less of the bread and milk and more of the soft food. At that point, gradually increase the soft food and cut down the bread and milk until the chicks are eating soft food only.

At this point, sprinkle the soft food with a little blue maw seed and soaked rape. The chicks will begin to peck at the seed and will develop a taste for it.

Soaked seed may now be given, but the supply of soft food should be continued. Chicks vary greatly over the weaning period, and it may be found that while some will take hard seed at eight weeks, others will not touch it until they are 10 weeks old. Do not be in too much of a hurry to wean the chicks on to hard seed. Supply it when the young are eight weeks old, and make absolutely sure that they are capable of taking it, and more importantly, of deriving benefit from it before taking away food to which they are accustomed.

The weaning process is one which is very worrying for Novices, but if the advice given is followed there should be little trouble. Take things gradually and easily, and the young birds will wean themselves almost automatically.

Two points must be borne in mind. When the decision to take the chicks away from their parents has been made and they have been removed, on no account should they be returned.

Some chicks will sit dejectedly on the floor of the flight making pathetic chirping noises and calling for food. The best advice is to ignore them, although at the same time keeping a watchful eye.

If, after some time, the chicks have made no attempt to take food, pick them up and wipe their beaks gently in the bread and milk. Do this several times, and eventually the bird will take food in its beak, following which it will very soon grasp the idea and will begin to feed itself.

At the age of 9–10 weeks, the young birds should be taking hard seed, and grit can then be introduced and the birds put on a normal diet.

Usually youngsters can be left with their parents until the next round of hatching, but should be separated with the new mating and nesting.

Cages used for weaning

When the chicks are removed from the aviaries of their parents, special requirements are necessary.

The food offered to the young chicks should be placed in open dishes where it can be seen. Obviously the food in open dishes is much more easily fouled by the droppings of the birds, with equally obvious results if it is not changed regularly

DIET FOR REARING THE CHICKS
(AN ALTERNATIVE)

On the day before the eggs are due to hatch, a small amount of soft food should be offered and continued thereafter. Some breeders do not believe in offering greenfood on the first day of hatching and withhold this until the chicks are three days old. Others believe that greenfood should be offered immediately the chicks have hatched.

The author's own view is that there is nothing wrong with either of these methods, and which one is chosen is a matter for the individual to decide. The cardinal rule of following a pattern which has been found to be successful applies here, and if the birds are content with the chosen method then by all means carry on using that method no matter what it may be.

Soft food should be supplied three times daily with a feed of bread and milk at mid-day if this is possible. Some breeders do not believe in giving bread and milk, but it is true to say that the larger majority of breeders do use this method on the assumption that bread and milk provides the hens with a food which is very easily converted to crop milk. The use of this method also accustoms the chicks to the food, which is an advantage during the time that they are being weaned away from their parents.

Soft food is usually offered in the morning, at tea time, and again just before dusk. The feed at dusk is of particular importance, the theory behind it being that the parents are tempted to feed by the introduction of fresh food into their cages and are more likely to feed the chicks just before they settle down for the night.

If soaked seed is to be given, then this should be offered from the first day of hatching.

LIGHTING

If, as has been suggested, the birds are hatching their eggs during the second week in April, the amount of light available to them and by which the young can be fed must be taken into consideration. It has already been seen that lighting is not essential in a bird room, but we must now consider whether it is desirable.

At this time of year, there are something of the order of twelve or thirteen hours of daylight. It is widely accepted that the birds need at least fourteen hours of daylight by which to rear their chicks, largely because when the chicks are very small, they will be quite unable to go through twelve hours of darkness without being fed. To counteract this twelve hour period of darkness, some breeders install automatic light switches.

WATER

Some fanciers do not believe in giving water for the first three days after the chicks have been placed in their weaning cages. The author's view is that clean fresh water never did any harm to any living creature and there is no reason to believe that it is bad for growing chicks.

When water is offered, it should be given by means of the fountain type of drinker which clips on the outside of the cage front and projects through the bars, the reason is the same as that of giving food in open dishes.

GOING LIGHT

A problem which may be encountered at this stage of the development of the chicks is that of 'going light', a term used to describe a physical condition in which they lose weight rapidly and the cause of which is unknown, although there are many theories on the subject.

When this condition occurs, there is rapid loss of weight and protrusion of the breast bone. The abdomen becomes distended and scaly, and any birds found to be in this condition should be isolated immediately. A pinch of permanganate of potash in 1 oz of drinking water should be given until the bird improves.

Another treatment for this condition, at least in theory, is that Glucose D should be added to the diet, mixed with the soft food. This is a very widely held belief and one to which many fanciers adhere very strongly indeed.

The most probable cause of this condition is a poorly balanced diet. It follows, therefore, that if this is the case then the provision of a well balanced diet should prevent the condition from arising.

THE SECOND ROUND

When the chicks from the first nest are 8 weeks old, the nest box should be taken down from the side of the house and placed in a corner, on the floor. A clean nest box and nesting material is then provided, whereupon the hen will begin to make her new nest when the first round chicks are about 9 weeks old. If this practice is not carried out the hen may well desert her first round chicks through paying more attention to the 'building' of her second nest. At this point, the cock should continue to feed the chicks.

There is the added problem that if the hen is anxious to start her second nest, she may well do so on top of the first round chicks and suffocate them, a situation which is by no means unknown.

When the hen has made her second nest, she will then lay her eggs and settle down to incubate them in the same way as she did with the first round, and the process of breeding management begins all over again.

Some breeders allow their hens to rear more than two rounds of chicks, but in the author's view, and that which is by far the most widely accepted, two rounds of chicks are quite enough for a hen to rear during any one breeding season. This is quite apart from the fact that if a third round should be reared, the young will almost certainly be in the nest during late July when the adult birds begin to moult, at which point they will probably lose interest in the chicks entirely and allow them to die.

If, for some reason, the first round has not been success-ful and no chicks have been reared from a particular pair, or perhaps only one chick, then it is acceptable to allow the pair to go to nest for a third time. If this situation arises, take care to work out the dates so that the pair are not left with young chicks in the nest when they begin to moult. Remember also, that the hen needs at least a little time to build up her strength between rearing her chicks and start-ing to moult.

BREEDING RECORDS

It is at the start of the incubation and particularly the point at which the chicks are removed from the cages of their parents that records must be carefully kept, and this is especially true if the aim is to begin the establishment of a line. It will also be to the advantage of the breeder to know how the pair brought up their young, what problems were encountered, how many eggs were laid, how many were fertile or infertile, the quality of the chicks produced from any given pair in terms of size, type and feather quality and any other records which the breeder might decide are important to the continuance of the line.

Many breeders claim to be able to look into a stock cage full of young chicks and to be absolutely certain in asserting that a particular chick came from a particular pair. This is very difficult to believe, especially where perhaps twenty birds, all of them clear, are concerned.

There is only one way to be absolutely sure on this point, and that is to place split celluloid rings on the legs of the chicks at the point at which they are removed from the cages of their parents. The rings are very easy to apply and will leave no doubt about which chick came from which pair.

The rings are put on by the use of a fluted metal tool which is supplied by the ring makers. The ring is pushed on to the tool until it opens sufficiently widely to slip easily over the leg of the chick between the ankle and the knee joint. The tool is then withdrawn and the ring will close around the leg. Many Novices are a little reticent about carrying out this operation, but it is really quite easily accomplished and can be completed very quickly indeed with a little practice. If the rings are put on, then the fancier will have no difficulty in identifying the birds when pairing up for the following breeding season and will be absolutely certain that his line breeding programme is going ahead as planned.

PROBLEMS IN THE BREEDING SEASON

There is absolute certainty that problems will be encountered. Rarely, if ever, does everything go as planned, and these remarks apply to expert and novice alike.

BREEDING ROOM REGISTER

PEN No. .... COCK .... HEN ....

First Egg Laid	Hen Set	Due to Hatch	No. of Young	Remarks

PEN No. .... COCK .... HEN ....

First Egg Laid	Hen Set	Due to Hatch	No. of Young	Remarks

Register which shows all essentials for each hen

Desertion

One problem which may be encountered is that of the hen deserting the nest. There are a variety of reasons for desertion, and one very common cause is the lack of an adequate supply of greenfood.

Many people have possibly reared chicks without offering greenfood at all, and would probably be of the opinion that the supply of such food is not essential. While this may be true in many cases, some breeding hens will certainly desert their young if adequate supplies of fresh greenfood are not offered.

Another cause of desertion is lack of privacy for the sitting hens.

Nest boxes should not be placed too close to the windows of the bird room where the hens are presented with external distractions which may frighten them and cause them to leave the nest.

Unusual noises both inside and outside the bird room should be completely eliminated during breeding operations and it would be true to say that there are many experienced fanciers who will not allow visitors into their bird rooms while breeding is in progress.

Another theory on the problems of desertion is that the birds are not being offered sufficient vitamin supplements. Whether this is true or not is a matter for debate. Many fanciers believe that if the ordinary diet is well balanced the birds will obtain all the vitamins they require. Other breeders give vitamin supplements at breeding time in order to make sure that the birds have a good and regular supply.

As we have already noted, the weather may also play a part in causing the hens to desert their chicks.

Hand rearing

Hand rearing is a very difficult and time consuming task, and although it would be true to say that chicks have been reared by hand, the chances of its succeeding are rather remote. If the hen has decided to desert the nest, then the first the fancier will know of it will be when he finds the chicks lying cold and obviously close to death in the bottom of the nest box.

If the chicks are found in this condition, then take

them in cupped hands and breathe hard on them. This will bring them back to normal body temperature relatively quickly, at which point the process of hand feeding can begin.

Make up some bread and milk in a very sloppy mixture and take a small syringe of the type used by doctors, but without the needle. Take the chick in the left hand, and gently stroke the yellow part of the back of the beak with the end of the syringe, whereupon the chick will gape for food. Insert only a little of the bread and milk mixture at a time, and when there is a reasonable amount of food in the crop, leave well alone. Give the chick plenty of time to pass the food into the crop before offering more. Forcing the food into the beak will result in blockage of the air passages and suffocation.

If this situation arises, the chicks should be fed every hour except at night when they can be left from the fall of darkness, after the final feed, until dawn.

Some breeders use a sharpened matchstick to carry out the same operation, and either method will suffice. The important point is to get food into the crop of the chick as quickly as possible under the conditions described and no matter what method is used to achieve this end, it is justified if it is effective.

If the hen does desert the nest, and the chicks can be brought back to the point at which they are sufficiently strong to gape for food in the normal manner, then they should be transferred to another nest of chicks of similar age if this is possible. A hen which has deserted her nest rarely returns to it, especially if the chicks have become weakened through lack of food. Under such circumstances there is a far greater possibility of their being reared by a foster hen than by their natural parents or by hand feeding.

One particular time at which hand feeding may be necessary is just before dusk, when the birds are beginning to settle down for the night. At that point, many breeders examine every nest and ensure that each chick has sufficient food in its crop, which can be very easily seen by looking at the translucent skin at the base of the neck. If the crop is empty then hand feeding must be attempted. If it is not, then the chances are that the chick will probably die of starvation during the night.

When young birds are hand-fed, egg is necessary as a

substitute for the secretion of the parental crop; and for the same reason the food should be given warm, for if cold when swallowed it is apt to cause distressing flatulence.

Suffocation of the chicks

Sometimes, the hen will sit so tightly on the nest that the chicks may be suffocated or crushed beneath her weight. This is especially true in dull and overcast weather conditions and under those conditions if may be better to leave the lights on in the bird room throughout the daylight hours.

This is a very difficult problem to solve, in that it the hen is constantly moved off the nest in an attempt to induce her to feed the chicks, she may eventually desert the nest entirely.   There is always the danger in these circumstances that if the hen does not leave the nest regularly she will obviously not be taking food and this will result in the starvation of the chicks and, in extreme cases, even of the hen herself.

So far as suffocation of the chicks is concerned, it is certainly very worthy of note that many fanciers leave any unhatched eggs in the nest until the chicks have reached a reasonable size.   This method has the effect of creating a space beneath the hen in which the very small chicks can find relief from her weight.

Problems with the cock

If the cock is doing his job correctly, he will help the hen by feeding her as she sits on the nest and may also feed the chicks at the later stages.

Sometimes the cock may be more interested in going to nest for the second round than in looking after the chicks and may well attack them and attempt to drive the hen to nest again.   If this situation arises the cock would be removed immediately and should not be allowed back with the hen until the chicks have been taken away from her.

Some breeders prefer to take the cock away in any event, whether he causes problems or not, on the assumption that if there are problems with rearing the chicks these are more likely to arise from the cock than from the hen. It would be true to say, however, that the majority of fanciers leave the cock with the hen because of the help he is able to give her in rearing the chicks and only remove him if he begins to cause trouble in the breeding cage.

RECENT OBSERVATIONS ON BREEDING

An experiment was carried out on the use of a plastic nest box. A used plastic drum was obtained and holes were cut in the side; then filled with earth and shavings to about 4 inches. The birds took to the nest immediately. Within two weeks they had laid an egg (early February) and by mid-March they had laid four eggs and the hen appeared to be sitting.

On examination of the nest when the hen was astride, it was found that a considerable number of feathers had been used both from the hen and the cock. The hen plucked all her breast feathers, but feathers were taken by both birds from each other because they appeared very raggy as if moulting — even off the back. The grey fluff was showing such was the extent of the plucking to line the nest.

A mistake made was to put too small a hole in the side with the result it was difficult to spot the hen on the nest. Also there was a problem in removing anything from the nest; checking the eggs was difficult.

Kakarikis are rather jumpy when nesting and, therefore, the minimum amount of disturbance is advised. Even when attempting routine feeding the hen seemed to be disturbed.

PRACTICAL POINTS

Questions raised by fanciers recently prompt this footnote on breeding:

1. **Age for breeding Kakarikis**
   They breed in their first year and quite regularly. As noted earlier, only two broods are recommended.
2. **Life Span of Kakarikis**
   Parrakeets normally live quite a long time, but various breeders have suggested that Kakarikis have a relatively short life span (, 2–3 years). One breeder has suggested that too many broods in a year may be the problem, weakening their constitution. Up to 10 years should be quite normal.

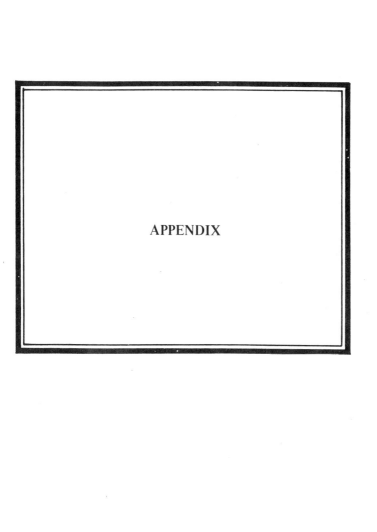

APPENDIX

APPENDIX

1. Sources of Supply

2. Parrot Society

3. Bibliography of main books consulted

4. Index

SOURCES OF SUPPLIES

Various companies and firms supply food and equipment
for cage birds and some of these are as follows (they are
also quoted in the text with appropriate equipment):

Bartholomews of Hampshire
Fyning, Rogate, West Sussex.
Tubular heaters, hospital cages, etc.

Haines Aviary Economy
28 Horsewell Lane, Wigston Magna, Leicester
Hoppers, Winnowing Machines, nest boxes, etc.

Shaws Pet Products Ltd
50 West Road, Aston Clinton, Aylesbury, Bucks
A wide range of supplements

Sinderins Electronic Products
Sheiron House, Memus, Forfar, DD8 3UA
Dimmers for controlled lighting

Prestige Technology Ltd
Thetford, Norfolk
Negative Air Ionisers for Birdrooms

Porters Pet Stores
81 Platchett Grove, London, E6
Cage fronts, show cages, foods and appliances

Ponderosa Bird Aviaries
The Reddings, Cheltenham, Glos.
Cages, food and various appliances

THE PARROT SOCIETY

Those interested in parrot-like birds are advised to join
The Parrot Society, 108b Fenlake Road, Bedford, MK42
0EU, England

BIBLIOGRAPHY

Many books and journals were consulted and in particular:

Kakarikis, I.S.Dyer, Isles d'Avon, Bristol, 1979
An interesting book which gives the experiences of the author in keeping Kakarikis. The emphasis is on the personal methods used and tried.

Parrots and Parrot-like Birds, Marquess of Tavistock
A pioneer aviculturist who believed that Kakarikis could be savage to other birds. Does not seem to fit in with modern experiences.

Encyclopaedia of Aviculture, A. Rutgers and K.A. Norris, Blandford Press, 1972
A large 3 volume set with volume 2 covering Parrots and Parrakeets.

Parrots, W.de Grahl, Ward Lock, 1981
A concise and very readable book on the Parrot Family.

Parrots, C.H. Rogers, Muller, 1953
A basic text for absolute beginners.

Foreign Bird Keeping, Iliffe, 1962

Parrots of the World, J.M. Forshaw, Landsdowne, Melbourne 1973
Very fine paintings by Wm. T. Cooper

The Foreigner, various dates
A magazine devoted to foreign bird keeping in the pre-1939 period.

The Avicultural Magazine various dates
Also bound copies of *Aviculture* isused by the Aviculture Society.

Cage and Aviary Birds, Reed Business Publishing
The main British magazine on aviculture and essential reading for all interested in cage birds.

INDEX

Puriri tree:13

Range of flights:60
Raoul Island:19
Raptorials:20
Red-Fronted New Zealand Parrakeets:5:8:10:11:24:25:29:34:36
Register. Breeding room:114
Reproduction:97
Reproduction System:91
Reproduction System-female:89
Ring-necked Parrakeet:2
Rose-breasted Cockatoo:2
Rosy-faced Lovebird:2
Ruahine Mountains:15
Rump:36

Second round:112
Seed hoppers:75
Seed-the importance of fresh:68
Seeds-mixed:80
Shell:92
Shrubs:58
Show cages:43
Side bands:36
Sifting seed:75
Size :35
Skeleton:86
Skeleton and Internal organs:87
Soaked-seed:75
Society Island Parrakeet (*Cyanoramphus nealandicus*):18
Sources of Supplies:22
Sparrow-hawk:20
Special Structures:58
Sprouting seeds:69:74
Steward Island:9:11
Strigopinae:3
Suffocation of chicks:117
Supplemented food:70

Tail:36
Tavistock.Marquess of *Parrots and Parrot-like Birds*:30
Toi-Toi:13
Tongue:4
Tubular heaters:48

Ulietea Island Parrakeet (*Cyanoramphus ulietanus*):18
Ulva's Island:16
Upper mandible:4

Ventilation:47

Waikaremoana Lake:11:15
Water:78:111

Water vessels:79
Weaning food, cages:108:109
Welfare:60
Wellington:14
Wings:36:87
White Cockatoo:11
Winnowing machine:77
Wooden Structures:60

Yellow-fronted Parrakeets:8:11:14:15:20:21:22:24:34:35

Zoological Society:8
Ziegensittich:12